IMPROVING ONLINE TEACHER EDUCATION

IMPROVING ONLINE TEACHER EDUCATION

Digital Tools and
Evidence-Based Practices

Rachel Karchmer-Klein

Foreword by Douglas Fisher

TEACHERS COLLEGE PRESS

TEACHERS COLLEGE | COLUMBIA UNIVERSITY
NEW YORK AND LONDON

Published by Teachers College Press,® 1234 Amsterdam Avenue, New York, NY 10027

Copyright © 2020 by Teachers College, Columbia University

Cover design by Patricia Palao. Cover image by hh5800 / iStock by Getty Images.

Library of Congress Cataloging-in-Publication Data is available at loc.gov

ISBN 978-0-8077-6368-1 (paper)
ISBN 978-0-8077-6369-8 (hardcover)
ISBN 978-0-8077-7847-0 (ebook)

Printed on acid-free paper
Manufactured in the United States of America

To my biggest fans, Joe and Ryan
And to my mom and dad, who would have been so proud

Contents

PART III: PUTTING IT TOGETHER

Foreword

When I ask most people about online learning, they either love it or hate it. When asked why, those who love it say that it is convenient and that they get to control the pace and place of their learning. Those who hate it report that it's hour after hour of independent learning with little or no help from the instructor. Having tutored many community college students, I can personally attest to the fact that there are many battery-operated worksheets out there. By that, I mean that there are tasks being assigned in a digital environment that are nothing more than low-level tasks that would have been photocopied and assigned to students in the past. How many of us have had an online learning experience in which we were asked to read or watch something and then perform some recall task, by ourselves, with that information? How many of us have engaged in online discussion boards in which the instructor never commented and only scored the fact that we posted? And how many of us have taken online quizzes by searching for the answers in another browser tab? Yes, there are any number of examples of ineffective online learning.

That's what makes this book, *Improving Online Teacher Education: Digital Tools and Evidence-Based Practices*, so exciting. There is knowledge, and a rather extensive evidence base, out there that shines a light on a better path for online learning. Unfortunately, most of us don't have that knowledge and, instead, we take what we thought worked in a live, face-to-face situation and try to retrofit it for online learning. As you engage with the ideas and information in this book, you'll come to understand the evidence that guided Rachel Karchmer-Klein as she wrote it.

As I was reading this book, I kept thinking that teacher educators should be the model for learning experiences, including online learning. The expectations, tasks, and assessment we give to our students should be shining examples of the possibilities that exist, if for no other reason than that our students will take the examples from their classes and use them with their students.

But I have a confession. I don't know all the latest apps, tools, and tricks, even though I try to keep up. I ask my students all the time, "What tool are you using?" and then I go and try them out. It's a lot of pressure to try to keep up. But your stress level will be reduced when you read this book. You don't need to know every tool. You just need to know the functionality you're looking for. As an example, if you want students to share information, there are any number of tools out there. By the time this book is in print, new tools will have been invented and older tools will have gone extinct. But, if you focus on the functionality, there will be a tool that works for you. In other words, it's a process. It's about using the medium (online, digital, and virtual) to convey the message. I can do that. And so can you.

It's time for a revolution in online learning. We should individually and collectively commit to providing our students—those who will eventually teach and lead in schools around the world—the best online learning experiences we can imagine. We should walk the talk and model the way. In doing so, we can deliver on the promise of online learning, which was to ensure that students had some control of the place, pace, and path of their learning. Everything you need to radically improve the online experience for your students is here for you. Turn the page and begin the journey.

—Douglas Fisher, San Diego State University

Acknowledgments

This work began in 2003 when I was given the freedom to teach my first fully online class at Virginia Commonwealth University. I want to thank the graduate students enrolled in that course and the many more who took online courses with me at the University of Delaware over the last 17 years. Their willingness to learn in new ways allowed me to strengthen my online teaching skills. I also want to thank the Office of Graduate and Professional Education and the School of Education at the University of Delaware for partially funding some of my online course development through a Provost's Initiative for Excellence and Innovation in E-Learning grant. I also want to thank my University of Delaware colleagues in the Master of Education in Teacher Leadership program who joined me in this online teaching journey. Their dedication to our program and graduate students has built our school's reputation in the area of online teaching and I am proud of what we've accomplished so far. In addition, I am grateful to Doug Fisher for connecting me with Jean Ward, my editor at Teachers College Press. Jean's supportive words and belief in me helped maintain my focus throughout this project. Thank you also to Heidi Anne Mesmer, my colleague for life. I am forever grateful our paths crossed in 1999. Your guidance through this experience was invaluable. And finally, a heartfelt thank you to my husband, Joe, and my son, Ryan, for cheering me on throughout this entire process. This book is as much theirs as it is mine given all the hours they sat patiently on the sidelines as I put words on these pages.

IMPROVING ONLINE TEACHER EDUCATION

Introduction

I taught my first fully online course in 2003 using Blackboard, the university's learning management system (LMS). The 7-week summer course focused on federally funded reading initiatives and incorporated a mix of asynchronous and synchronous online activities. At the time Reading First, a federally funded education program encouraging the use of scientifically based reading research as the foundation for early literacy instruction, had generated many books in the market that shared varying perspectives of the legislation. With the goal of fostering thoughtful class conversations, I chose two books written by authors with contrasting views. The asynchronous sessions were organized as literature circles, where graduate students were divided into groups and assigned roles to facilitate conversations about the texts by interacting on group discussion boards using written language. The synchronous portions brought the students together to discuss the books with their authors in real time using a chat tool, again with written language.

Compared to today, those author chats were archaic. Imagine this: I'm sitting at my computer in Philadelphia. My students are at their homes in Virginia. My first guest speaker was in Chicago. We are all using dialup and text chat to communicate. There is no audio or video. I begin the conversation by introducing the speaker, outlining the guidelines for the chat, and then calling on the first student to type a question. Next, we all wait, for what feels like forever, for the author to respond. The process repeats itself until all fifteen students ask a question. It is a painfully slow experience. Nevertheless, after class, students express appreciation for the opportunity to talk directly with the author.

Although cumbersome, this chat sparked my interest in designing more online teaching opportunities for my teacher education courses. At the time, new technologies were constantly emerging. Students were becoming more comfortable with different devices. And, importantly, technology was gaining traction as a requirement of teacher preparation.

Instead of only modeling how to integrate technology into my students' future K–12 instruction, I was determined to use it regularly in my own college-level teaching.

More than 17 years later, I continue to design and teach online under-graduate- and graduate-level courses in literacy, teacher leadership, and educational technology. I also design online professional development for state education departments, coordinate two exclusively online graduate teacher education programs, and support colleagues across the country in their online program and course development endeavors. Each of these experiences has taught me a lot, but perhaps the most impactful lesson has been to see how challenging it is for instructors to create meaningful collegial interactions online: that is, opportunities for classmates to share ideas and practices, problem-solve, and participate productively through collaborative and interactive activities in online environments. It was this particular challenge that led me to write this practical guide for university educators tasked with teaching online.

Collaboration in digital spaces means creating shared learning experiences (Karpova, Correia, & Baran, 2009). *Interactivity* refers to users exchanging ideas and alternative perspectives (Castek, Beach, Cotanch, & Scott, 2014) with a variety of modes. Most LMSs provide a range of digital tools, such as discussion boards, peer review applications (apps), and video conferencing, that can be leveraged to design collegial interactions both asynchronously and synchronously. In turn, students can seamlessly connect with classmates, instructors, and content, as well as people outside of the course (e.g., experts in the field).

WHY TEACHER EDUCATION?

Those who teach teachers should be pedagogical experts, yet many have little or no experience implementing evidence-based practices (EBP) within digital environments. I certainly didn't until I spent hours researching and practicing how to use different tools to create digital learning opportunities that led to student learning. Teacher education courses tend to incorporate assignments such as case study analysis, lesson plan design, and reflection on practice more than didactic delivery that assesses student knowledge through multiple-choice tests. In my experience, designing engaging instruction for online environments is time-consuming and requires a combination of pedagogical and technological skills.

ASSUMPTIONS

A friend of mine was taking a 7-week online course in computer science, and we met at the end of the semester to discuss his experience. He explained that the weekly modules focused on different topics, and students learned the content by completing the cycle of activities shown in Figure I.1.

By the second week of class he realized that the video lecture mirrored the textbook, so he would begin by watching the lecture and refer to the book only if he didn't understand a concept. Next, he would complete the quiz and post a response to a prompt on the class discussion board, but he rarely, if ever, read classmates' comments or interacted with them, because the professor didn't require them to do so. He told me he learned a lot of content but said, "I would've learned just as much if I bought the textbook and read it on my own." To me, this was a disappointing assessment in light of the high cost of higher education as well as the time and effort it takes to pursue a graduate degree.

While the didactic online course delivery my friend experienced may work for some instructors and students, it is not the approach taken here. The content shared in this book emphasizes collaborative and interactive instructional design framed by the following five assumptions.

Figure I.1. Cycle of Activities in Online Computer Science Course

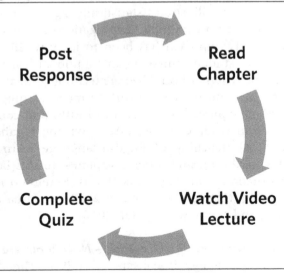

Assumption 1: Instructional Design Is Paramount

Online teaching is not just translating face-to-face instruction into digital delivery. It requires carefully constructing activities that leverage technology to meet the needs of diverse learners. To this end, the three tenets described below inform my thinking as I follow a recursive, sometimes complicated, process of designing online activities.

Fit Tools to the Task. First, learning objectives are prioritized. The initial step is always to identify exactly what it is I want students to know and then choose technology tools that can facilitate learning. Although this may seem obvious, most technology preparation opportunities for teachers focus on the how-to of digital tools (Harris & Hofer, 2009) and skim over instruction about using them to meet curricular goals. This leads to lessons built around what the technology can do rather than what the teacher hopes to accomplish. However, when instructional design begins with a focus on learning goals, teachers frame their pedagogical decisions and technology selections around them (Hutchison & Woodward, 2014).

Use and Model Evidence-Based Practices. Second, just as we teach our students that instruction must be evidence-based (Scheeler, Budin, & Markelz, 2016), so too must our online practices be. This is tricky, as there is little research in online education (U.S. Department of Education, 2010) that illustrates statistically significant increases in student performance across multiple investigations (Graham, Harris, & Chambers, 2016). My approach has been to identify EBPs that have evidence of positive student outcomes in traditional learning settings and then determine whether I can leverage technological affordances to integrate those EBPs into my coursework to meet learning objectives. For years I have maintained a running list of EBPs that come from reviews of research in reading (Israel, 2017), writing (Graham, Harris, & Chambers, 2016), teaching of English-language learners (Fitton, McIlraith, & Wood, 2018), and other disciplines. In this book I share examples of instruction framed by think alouds (Bereiter & Bird, 1985), case-based learning (Ertmer & Koehler, 2018), field-based practice (Zeichner, 2012), and peer coaching (Lu, 2010).

Don't Wed Activities to Specific Tools—New Tools are Constantly Emerging. Third, technology is constantly in flux. The devices and applications of today can easily be replaced by new, faster, more creative versions tomorrow. However, if learning drives instructional design, then course activities do not become wedded to a specific tool. Instead, they can easily be adapted to different apps, which may enable new ways of achieving the same student understandings.

Assumption 2: Instructional Design Should Be Informed by Cognitive, Social, and Situated Learning Perspectives

From a cognitive perspective, learning is guided by underlying mental processes, like when we connect new ideas and concepts to existing understandings or monitor comprehension as we read a text (Tracey & Morrow, 2017). From a social perspective, knowledge is constructed through ongoing and collaborative experiences with others (Vygotsky, 1978). A situated learning perspective (Herrington & Oliver, 2000) informs instruction by infusing authentic contexts into coursework and showing how knowledge can be applied to real life experiences. The affordances of digital tools create rich avenues for learners to acquire knowledge independently while also exploring content with classmates. The modules in this book demonstrate how to use technology to combine electronic resources with EBPs in ways that draw upon these perspectives, ensuring students have a variety of opportunities to master and apply concepts.

Assumption 3: Four Unique Attributes of Digital Text Must Be Leveraged Intentionally

All digital tools, including LMSs (e.g., Sakai, Blackboard, Canvas), share a common medium, digital text, characterized by four attributes:

- Digital texts are *multimodal*: they encompass a variety of modes, signs, and symbols that communicate meaning (e.g., images, sounds).
- Digital texts are *malleable*, allowing authors to continuously revise written language, images, and design, even after publication.
- Digital texts are many times *nonlinear*, such as when hyperlinks are integrated to guide readers to different sources or aspects of the same text.
- Digital text is used to communicate over the Internet, affording readers and writers opportunities to *collaborate* and *interact*.

In sum, no matter the subject, learning objective, or length of a course, digital text can be used to deliver content in a variety of ways. However, in order to do so effectively, course designers must be aware of the attributes outlined above: multimodality, malleability, nonlinearity, and interactivity (Jewitt, 2014).

Assumption 4: Educators Teach Online for Different Reasons

The movement toward online program and course delivery has notably strengthened in the field of teacher education (Butrymowicz, 2012; Karchmer-Klein & Pytash, 2020). For instance, in 2018 *US News and World Report* identified 247 public and private institutions of higher education that offered completely online graduate programs in education. I am fortunate in that my turn toward online teaching was not forced by administrative directives. However, it would be remiss to ignore that many faculty members are told their courses must be offered online (Allen & Seaman, 2016).

Assumption 5: Teacher Educators Model Technology Integration for Their Students

Education associations have developed content-area standards that recognize the role of digital literacies within K–12 instruction (e.g., International Society for Technology in Education, 2016; National Council for the Social Studies, 2016; National Council of Teachers of English, 2018). For instance, digital competencies for teachers to master are embedded throughout the International Literacy Association's recently published *Standards for the Preparation of Literacy Professionals 2017* (ILA, 2018). Teachers must be able to use a variety of digital materials to engage and motivate learners, build knowledge collaboratively, transform their teaching, and support colleagues in learning to use a range of digital tools. Thus, instructors who deliver a course online are well positioned to model digital literacies to ensure teacher education standards are met by coursework. In my face-to-face undergraduate literacy course, for instance, I start every class with a read-aloud with a theme related to the day's topic. I model fluent reading practices (Hudson, Lane, & Pullen, 2011) and envelop the class in the story so it becomes a shared reading experience (Neuman & Dickinson, 2011). Similarly, in all my online courses, I couple a range of EBPs with the types of technologies currently used in K–12 instruction, such as FlipGrid, Padlet, ShowMe, and VoiceThread.

WHY THIS BOOK?

Several years ago, I took a course in online teaching offered by my university. My classmates were faculty with a range of technology skills who taught across campus in departments including business, human resources, fashion design, and urban studies. Although some of the technical aspects reviewed were practical, since we had migrated to a new LMS (e.g., how to insert images), the teaching examples shared ranged widely, making it difficult to situate them within my own discipline. This experience reinforced my sense of the importance of designing a practical guide on a particular field for a particular audience.

I recognize readers of this text have varying levels of skill and interest in technology-integrated instruction. For this reason, the book is organized non-sequentially so they can choose the topics and activities most relatable and useful to their professional environment. The final chapter of this text invites readers to build a digital professional learning network (PLN), where they can explore areas of tech integration related to specific interests and problems of practice.

This book sets itself apart from similar texts in three ways. First, because all my online experience has been in teacher education, I share illustrative examples taken directly from the field. The content is applicable to a variety of situations and content areas in education (e.g., literacy, math, educational leadership) so that readers can design their own quality learning opportunities for students. Second, unlike many published texts, I do not attempt to cover every aspect of online teaching and learning. Instead, I focus on developing collaborative and interactive experiences by leveraging digital tools using evidence-based practices. Third, my intention is to provide a space that encourages readers to interact with the content by brainstorming and creating as they progress through its pages. My hope is to show engaging and productive ways to teach any and all content online that will make the process more satisfying even for instructors for whom teaching online may not be a choice or a priority.

BOOK ORGANIZATION

As a practical guide for teacher educators who teach online, the contents of this book are organized into three parts and designed to be used to directly support course design and implementation. Throughout the text I refer to graduate and undergraduate students as *candidates*, rather than students, and reserve the term *students* for K–12 students. Additionally, the examples shared refer to the LMS Canvas since it is the tool I have used most in the last 10 years.

Framing Online Course Design

Part I draws upon theory and research to present a framework to conceptualize instructional design for online environments. Chapter 1 describes the attributes of digital text and takes the reader through a series of activities to build awareness of them. Chapter 2 introduces the pedagogy of multiliteracies (Cope & Kalantzis, 2015) and explains how four knowledge processes (experiencing, conceptualizing, analyzing, and applying) can be used to frame the design of effective online instruction.

Developing Evidence-Based Online Instruction

Part II provides readers with concrete examples of using technology to integrate evidence-based teaching practices into online coursework. Chapter 3 illustrates how to incorporate digital think alouds into teacher education. Chapter 4 details how to use digital tools to implement case-based instructional opportunities. Chapter 5 spotlights the EBP of peer feedback, and Chapter 6 focuses on how to use digital affordances to design a virtual version of traditional field-based practices, not to replace site-based student teaching but to enrich online professional courses. Each chapter concludes with a dedicated space for readers to design a series of activities implementing the EBP described in that chapter. The text scaffolds the process with prompts to identify learning objectives and digital resources that will let candidates experience, conceptualize, analyze, and apply content within a particular context.

Putting the Pieces Together

Part III brings the content from the previous chapters together by providing a framework for the long-term preparation behind designing an entire course. The book concludes by highlighting a range of principles to keep in mind when making instructional decisions such as differentiating instruction, respecting diversity, and participating in ongoing professional development. The final part of this text also acknowledges the need for ongoing support as readers embark on the journey toward online instruction.

Each chapter includes education-related examples detailing directions and applications of digital tools for learning activities; student work excerpts to illustrate potential outcomes of activities; and lessons learned as an online instructor along the way. It is important to note that all activities shared in this text can be tailored toward a range of education programs and academic levels. I've also included other instructors' and candidates' voices to highlight additional perspectives on the challenges and positive outcomes of online practices.

Additional Resources Online

It is difficult to present multimodal ideas within the pages of a printed book, so I created a companion website where readers can find additional resources related to the topics covered here. There is also a blog where I will reflect on my online teaching by sharing new ideas, discuss successful and failed attempts at new lessons, and post lists of digital tools I think benefit student learning in teacher preparation. The website is: improvingonlineteachered.com.

CONCLUSION

Overall, it is my hope that readers of this book will find new approaches to reconceptualizing teaching in ways that leverage the powerful affordances of the most current technologies, will grow more comfortable in using them, and will see greater interactivity, engagement, and success.

Part I

FRAMING OF
ONLINE INSTRUCTION

CHAPTER 1

Digital Text

> If our schools continue to limit the literacy curriculum to reading and writing traditional, alphabetic, printed texts, then our children will be well prepared for 1950 but ill prepared for 2050. (Baker, Pearson, & Rozendal, 2010, p. 2)

I've posted this quote on the opening slide of many professional development presentations over the years. It sparks rich conversation about current literacy practices and debate about instructional priorities. Like Baker, Pearson, and Rozendal (2010), I believe we are doing a disservice to educators and students when we do not expand how we teach reading, writing, listening, and speaking skills to include *digital literacies*, "the ability to use information and communication technologies to find, evaluate, create, and communicate information, requiring both cognitive and technical skills" (American Library Association, 2013). Although technology access and use in K–12 classrooms has increased dramatically in the last 20 years, most published literacy curriculum continues to focus on traditional conceptions of reading and writing (Mills & Exley, 2014). This results in K–12 students only being taught to read left to right and top to bottom using static, one-dimensional resources (Jewitt, 2014).

But let's take a step back. For classroom teachers to reconceptualize literacy instruction, teacher educators must be aware of digital literacy skills so they can define, model, and provide opportunities for candidates to engage with them. This is especially true for teacher educators who teach online.

I'm sure you've heard the saying, "All teachers are teachers of reading." I say that all online instructors, no matter the discipline, must be teachers of *digital text*, the medium used to communicate through digital technologies. If you design online courses, you must know how to leverage the attributes of digital text to design cohesive, dynamic online instruction. Moreover, you must be able to support students in their navigation of your courses so they get the most benefit.

This chapter describes the attributes of digital text. It also engages readers in a series of activities to strengthen awareness of different literacy skills necessary to design and navigate online environments.

ATTRIBUTES OF DIGITAL TEXT

If you are teaching online in any capacity (e.g., hybrid, fully online, asynchronous, synchronous), you are using digital text. Digital texts have several attributes that set them apart from traditionally printed text. First, they are *multimodal*. This means they consist of more than one *mode*, which is a sign or symbol that communicates meaning. Written and oral language, audio, images (moving or still), and hyperlinks are examples of modes (Cope & Kalantzis, 2015). *Modal affordances* are the ways in which we use modes to create sensory experiences central to meaning-making (Massumi, 2002). For instance, font size and color are affordances of written language. Loud, fast, or soft music are audio affordances.

A second attribute of digital text is that it is *malleable*. This means it can be easily added, revised, or deleted. As an online instructor, I find the malleability of digital text to be a benefit, especially if I find mistakes in my coursework or I need to modify instruction mid-semester to better meet my candidates' learning needs.

Digital text has the potential to be *nonlinear*. I say potential because it depends on how it is designed by the producer of the text. For instance, in my online courses, I encourage candidates to follow a linear sequence as they work through each module because my design is such that each activity builds upon the prior one. Yet the digital text is still nonlinear in that I can include hyperlinks to online resources or other sections of the course within each activity. When designing online courses, instructors must think carefully about how candidates will navigate the resources used in the class. This is especially true if, as in my courses, activities must be done in a particular sequence.

A fourth attribute of digital text is the *collaboration* and *interactivity* it affords the user. I delineate collaboration and interactivity in that collaboration happens when candidates work together to complete the same task. For example, Twiddla (www.twiddla.com/) is a multiuser whiteboard app. Candidates can meet up on the app in real time and brainstorm, draft, and collaborate on class activities. Google Docs (www.google.com/docs/about/) is another multiuser tool, where candidates can compose

ATTRIBUTES OF DIGITAL TEXT	
Multimodal	More than one sign or symbol to communicate meaning
Malleable	Easily added, revised, or deleted
Nonlinear	Nonsequential
Collaborative	Working with others to complete the same task
Interactive	Inviting others to provide feedback and alternative perspectives

documents individually or as a group in real time or asynchronously. Interactivity, on the other hand, invites others to provide feedback and alternative perspectives. Discussion boards, for instance, are probably the most commonly used digital tool in online classes for promoting interactivity. Professors assign a reading or video and ask candidates to respond to a prompt. These activities are then followed by candidates commenting on classmates' responses. Other digital tools that foster interactivity in this way include VoiceThread (voicethread.com) and Poll Everywhere (www.polleverywhere.com/).

BUILDING KNOWLEDGE OF DIGITAL TEXT

We assume that since most people use digital tools regularly, they understand these attributes of digital text. Yet it takes just a few moments to think of examples of how users could improve their skills. Here are a few mistakes that are familiar to many:

- Forwarding an email that wasn't meant to be sent to others
- Sending a GIF that was misconstrued by the recipient
- Getting lost on the Internet when you click too many hyperlinks
- Not realizing that modes other than words may convey meaning

I have found the most effective way to learn about digital text is to *build awareness* of its attributes, *analyze* the attributes separately and then in combination, and *apply* this knowledge to professional contexts. The next section of this chapter presents a series of short activities to scaffold understanding of the role of digital text in online coursework.

Activity 1: Frequency Count

Learning Objective: Notice modes and your interpretation of them as a consumer of digital text.

- Go to Glogpedia, a website that lets users create online posters: edu.glogster.com/glogpedia.
- Choose a glog of interest to you.
- Count the number of different modes on the poster. These may include written words, video, audio, images (still and moving), and hyperlinks.
- Did the modes used most frequently support your understanding of the poster's meaning, or distract you?

Activity 2: Modal Affordances

Learning Objective: Consider the effects of modal affordances.

- Go to www.youtube.com/watch?v=F2bk_9T482g
- Turn *off* the sound and watch the scene from the movie *Up* by Pixar.
- Turn *on* the sound and watch the scene again.
- Compare the two presentations of the same video and consider whether and how the music advances the narrative.

Activity 3: Making Meaning from a Digital Multimodal Narrative

Learning Objective: Analyze your meaning-making from a digital multimodal narrative.

- Go to *Inanimate Alice: Episode 1 China*: www.inanimatealice.com/episode1/
- Watch Episode 1.
- Watch Episode 1 again and answer the following
  - » Why do you think the music begins on the third frame?
  - » Why do you think the arrows appear on the road in frame six instead of close to the text? What effect does it have on your reading?

» Examine the screen when Alice writes things she'd rather be doing. Does Alice sound like an 8-year old? Why?

» Examine the final two screens of the story. How is the story's ending realized in the modes? What effect do the modes have on your understanding of the story?

Activity 4: Reading Path

Learning Objective: Document and analyze your reading path as you read an informational website.

- Select a screen capture tool (see Chapter 3 for description and tools).
- Select a website on an unfamiliar topic.
- Turn on screen capture tool and record a think aloud of your reading path as you navigate the website. Use the cursor to represent your eye movement and the order in which you read the content.
- Watch the recording and identify:
  » Your first action upon opening the website
  » Modes you relied upon for meaning of the content
  » Modes you ignored
  » Overall path you followed; for example, top to bottom, left to right, no pattern

Activity 5: Identifying Differences

Learning Objective: Compare and contrast two digital versions of the same story.

- Read/view the online versions of the classic folk tale, *The City Mouse and the Country Mouse,* indicated in Table 1.1.
- As you read/view each, record the modes used and describe how each mode is used to convey meaning on Table 1.1.
- Think about the affordances of the modes and how each mode contributes to the presentation of the story.
- Review the completed chart and compare and contrast the two versions.

Table 1.1. Compare and Contrast Chart

Version 1: *The City Mouse and the Country Mouse* at **bygosh.com** www.bygosh.com/ Features/082000/mouse.htm		Version 2: *City Mouse and Country Mouse* **at PBS Learning Media:** whyy.pbslearningmedia.org/ resource/btl10.ela.early. citymouseandcountrymouse/ city-mouse-and-country-mouse/	
Mode	**How is this mode used to convey meaning in the story?**	**Mode**	**How is this mode used to convey meaning in the story?**

Activity 6: Collaborate

Learning Objective: Co-construct knowledge with at least one other person and analyze the malleability of digital text.

- Identify one or more teacher educators to work with you on this activity.
- Read the following articles:
  - » Marshall, R. F. (2016). Why our daughter isn't opting out of state tests. *Newsday.* Retrieved from www.newsday.com/ opinion/why-my-daughter-won-t-opt-out-of-state-tests-in-new-york-1.11635872
  - » Goodman, J. (2015). You're wrong about Common Core math: Sorry, parents, but it makes more sense than you

think. *Salon*. Retrieved from www.salon.com/2015/11/28/ youre_wrong_about_common_core_math_sorry_parents_ but_it_makes_more_sense_than_you_think/

- Work as a group to create a statement to be shared with novice teachers who are confronted by parents and students outraged over state testing.
- Brainstorm, draft, and finalize your statement using Google Docs or another writing collaboration tool.
- Once finished, review the changes to the document.
  » If you used Google Docs in Google Chrome, download the Chrome Extension *Draftback*. This is an application that allows you to play back a Google Doc's revision history. Watch the revision history for your collaborative writing.
- Consider the following questions:
  » What do you notice about the malleability of the text?
  » Did one person make more changes than the other collaborator(s)?
  » Was your writing revised by a collaborator? If so, how did you feel about it?

Activity 7: Try It Out

Learning Objective: Apply what you learned about digital text and invite interactivity.

- Choose an article from one of the classes you teach.
- Choose a digital tool to create a digital text.
  » 30hands: 30hands.com/
  » Toontastic 3D: toontastic.withgoogle.com/
  » Explain Everything: explaineverything.com/
  » Soundtrap: www.soundtrap.com/
  » VoiceThread: voicethread.com/
- Design a digital multimodal presentation. The content of the multimodal composition should be organized around the 3-2-1 framework in response to the article you selected.
  » 3 things you learned
  » 2 questions you have about the article
  » 1 approach to applying what you learn to your professional setting
  » Keep in mind:
    ✓ Choose modes that reflect your message

✓ Consider your reader's path
✓ Each digital tool has its own affordances and constraints. For instance, Soundtrap will tell your story through audio only.

- Share your presentation with others and invite constructive comments on the design and content of the presentation

SUMMARY

Online instructors must be mindful of the attributes of digital text. This is critical at the course design stage. It is also important once the course is in full swing so instructors can provide support to candidates as they interact with the modules and their classmates. The activities presented here provide just a few opportunities to become aware of, analyze, and apply digital literacy skills. I encourage readers to complete them as well as assign them to online candidates to help prepare for online coursework and the integration of digital texts into their own teaching.

CHAPTER 2

Setting the Stage

The most important thing for me as an online student was the organization of the course. In my favorite classes the content of each module built upon or related to one another. Then within each module there were varied opportunities to learn content and express my thinking.

—Maureen McDonald, EdD Candidate

Recently I was invited to sit on a panel with colleagues from other units at my university to discuss online teaching. I was one of four presenters to discuss the challenges confronted when transitioning to online delivery of coursework from face-to-face instruction. During the question-and-answer portion of this presentation, the topic of design came up repeatedly. How do you decide on the activities included in your courses? Do you suggest a certain sequence of activities? How do you design active creative instruction? What does it look like? I wasn't surprised by this line of questioning. In fact, I was glad it came up because course design was a topic I grappled with for many years and one with which I feel much more comfortable now.

Lately, conversations about technology-integrated instruction have shifted from *whether* technology should be used in learning to *how* it can be used to offer students high-quality educational experiences (U.S. Department of Education, 2016). Moreover, it is clear that it is the instructional design of a lesson that leads to effective technology-infused learning opportunities, not the digital tools themselves (Beach & O'Brien, 2015; Castek & Beach, 2013).

This chapter presents my *how*, the design framework I share with colleagues inside and outside of my university in answer to the kinds of questions posed above. It defines the types of activities instructors should draw upon in each module of coursework to provide candidates with seamless, organized learning opportunities like the ones the student mentions in the quote above. I share this framework because I know it is useful. I studied it when conducting research on iPad integration in middle school disciplinary instruction (Karchmer-Klein, Mouza, Shinas, & Park,

2017). I apply it to my course design regularly, and I share it with other educators whenever I have the opportunity.

PEDAGOGY OF MULTILITERACIES

In 1994, the New London Group (NLG), a collective of international literacy researchers, met to discuss the ways literacy was evolving in response to new technologies, social diversity, and globalization. The publication *A Pedagogy of Multiliteracies: Designing Social Futures* (New London Group, 1996) identified the term *multiliteracies* to represent the growing "multiplicity of communication channels" (p. 63). As it pertained to technology, multiliteracies theory highlighted the complexities of digital texts and the need to prepare readers and writers of all content areas to effectively make meaning from and with them. Additionally, the members of the NLG were interested in not only what skills students needed to learn to effectively navigate online spaces, but also how teaching environments could foster rich, dynamic learning experiences.

Cope and Kalantzis (2015) refined the NLG's initial realization of the pedagogy of multiliteracies. Instead of didactic pedagogy where content is transmitted from teacher to student, or authentic pedagogy that reflects situated learning opportunities, they recommend *reflexive* pedagogy, a combination of didactic and authentic pedagogies that engages students in a mix of digital and nondigital activities based upon content, learning contexts, and student needs.

Cope and Kalantzis (2015) recommend educators design instruction encompassing four processes that reflect ways that knowledge is constructed: experiencing, conceptualizing, analyzing, and applying. *Experiencing* is the introduction of new ideas and the extension of prior knowledge. Activities that support this dimension may require students to describe, explore, predict, and examine content. Learners are actively involved when they *conceptualize*, which is the act of making mental and theoretical connections between concepts. They may hypothesize, problem-solve, estimate, or classify content. *Analyzing* refers to drawing upon prior content and experiences to think critically about them. Students may make conclusions, judge information, and critique resources when they engage in these activities. *Applying* is the transfer to and utilization of knowledge in real-world contexts. This may be done through composing, planning, illustrating, or constructing representations of their learning. Table 2.1 presents examples of activity types related to the topic of classroom behavior management.

Table 2.1. Knowledge Processes and Sample Activities

Learning Objective	Knowledge Process	Sample Activities
Candidates will understand and apply approaches to behavior management in K–12 classrooms.	Experiencing	Conduct Internet research to identify at least four types of behavior management strategies.
	Conceptualizing	Compare and contrast two types of behavior management strategies.
	Analyzing	Read at least two examples of each behavior management strategy in practice and identify your own beliefs about how to manage behavior in the classroom.
	Applying	Watch a video case study of a classroom in need of behavior management. Present your position on how the issues could be resolved.

These four knowledge processes are not separate or sequential do-mains. Rather, they should be interwoven throughout a series of activities to provide students with varied cross-disciplinary learning opportunities in digital spaces (Cazden, 2006). Research indicates a combination of these knowledge processes can innovate content and support student learning (Karchmer-Klein et al., 2017).

APPROACHES TO ONLINE INSTRUCTIONAL DESIGN

As discussed in Chapter 1, digital texts and the tools we use to communicate through them have a range of attributes that can be leveraged within instructional design. These include multimodality, collaboration, and interactivity. I reiterate the importance of these because they must be considered during the brainstorming, drafting, and crafting of online lessons. For instance, after identifying the learning objective, you may want students to collaborate on one or more activities. If so, you will need to consider at which point of the lesson you will want to bring candidates together and which digital tools will be used to facilitate collaboration.

In the next section I describe four approaches to creating an instructional chain, a sequence of activities designed to meet the same learning objectives (VanDerHeide & Newell, 2013). This pathway, framed by the four knowledge processes, provides context when making pedagogical decisions about how to structure online course design.

Beginning with Experiencing

As we teach our candidates, it is useful to tap into background knowledge prior to introducing new information or extending what is already known about a topic. Therefore, it isn't surprising that most instructional chains in online coursework begin with experiencing new or known information. The multimodal affordances of an LMS make it easy to embed video simulations, podcasts, electronic games, or online readings directly into the first content page of a module. This approach positions the candidate as a consumer of knowledge, learning information from the resources the instructor selected to begin the lesson. You could also flip the design and put candidates in the role of producer. As in a KWL (Ogle, 1986), candidates could be asked to write what they know about a topic in the LMS discussion board or post a note in Padlet, an online collaborative bulletin board, in response to a prompt provided by the instructor. These kinds of activities build community as candidates co-construct foundational knowledge before they dive into a lesson.

Applying Knowledge

In preparation for this book, I reviewed my online instruction to identify themes in my design. One element stood out to me. I always require candidates to apply content knowledge at some point in an instructional chain. When I examined my lessons further, I realized this was possible because, like most teacher education courses, I require some level of situated learning. In some instances, I provide case studies which virtually place candidates within different professional situations. They can then apply what they've learned to problem-solve or make recommendations based on the cases, for example. Other instances are more organic. The undergraduate educational technology and differentiated instruction courses I teach require a field placement in local elementary classrooms, and my graduate-level courses require candidates to work in or have access to education-related professional settings. Because I can count on access to schools, I assign activities that require candidates to write case studies of their own experiences, illustrating how they apply content knowledge learned in class to their professional settings. Overall, application of content in teacher education courses can invite a host of possibilities when designing creative online activities.

Multiple Activity Types

Instructional chains (VanDerHeide & Newell, 2013) are typically three or more sequential activities that are designed to meet the same learning objectives in different ways, perhaps through varying modalities or different degrees of depth. As I would for face-to-face instruction, once the learning objectives are assigned to a module, I begin to brainstorm how I want to teach the content, how I want candidates to learn the content, and how I will assess candidate understanding. Structuring my course design with instructional chains in mind helps me think about where I want to begin and end in each module.

There are two ways to think about the actual activities you assign to candidates. One approach is combining digital and non-digital activities. The other is creating instructional chains that require candidates to utilize only digital sources throughout the learning process. Below, I describe both and provide examples.

Digital and Non-Digital Activities. Just because a course is delivered online does not mean all activities must take place there. For instance, candidates may learn more about experiments in science methods courses if they conduct them with actual manipulatives rather than virtual simulations. In fact, I had a colleague who taught an online course in astronomy. She would change the content of her course depending upon which constellations and planets could be seen in the night sky during the semester she was teaching. She explained that she would rather her students observe the actual stars and planets from outside their own homes than watch a video online.

Table 2.2 is an example of an instructional chain implemented in a content area literacy course. It incorporates both digital and non-digital activities.

All-Digital Activities. Of course, the online course does lend itself to integrating a variety of digital tools for learning. All-digital instructional chains can provide students with opportunities to consume digital content from multiple sources, produce digital texts to represent their learning, and interact or collaborate with others through digital communication channels. This practice is called app-smashing, when more than one technology tool is used to complete an instructional chain (Kulowiec, 2013). Table 2.3 illustrates a lesson that uses all digital activities to teach candidates to identify effective literacy instruction for English Language Learners. A description of all digital tools referenced in this text can be found in Appendix B.

Table 2.2. Example of Digital and Non-Digital Instructional Design

Learning Objective(s)	Activities	Knowledge Processes	Digital Tools	Attributes of Digital Text
Candidates examine the topic of social capital in schools and examine its role in their professional settings.	Watch video lecture	Experience	LMS	Multimodality
	Read articles	Experience	LMS	Multimodality
	Rate Yourself as a Team Player	Apply		
	Survey colleagues at professional setting and reflect on findings as a team	Apply/ Analyze		
	Report findings to class	Analyze	LMS Discussion Board	Interactivity, Multimodality

Table 2.3. Example of All-Digital Instructional Design

Learning Objective(s)	Activities	Knowledge Processes	Digital Tools	Attributes of Digital Text
Candidates will identify and conceptualize elements of effective instruction for English Language Learners.	Watch video lecture	Experience	LMS	Multimodality
	Watch videos of ELL instruction	Experience	Teaching Channel/ LMS	Multimodality
	Identify elements of effective instruction	Apply	FlipGrid	Multimodality/ Interactivity
	Categorize approaches to instruction by type	Conceptualize	Popplet	Multimodality
	Share mind map with classmates and compare and contrast findings.	Analyze/ Apply	LMS Discussion Board	Multimodality/ Interactivity

Designing Your Own

Online instructional design takes a great deal of time and effort. I've found it is more time intensive than design for my in-person classes because my entire course is published for candidates on the first day of class. This makes it imperative I think through the lessons carefully so that I design a seamless experience where each activity builds upon the next.

If you are new to online design or would like to increase your skills, I recommend completing the following activity. It invites you to translate a non-digital lesson into one that integrates technology.

First, select a face-to-face lesson with multiple steps that you have already taught and you consider to be well designed. Next, fill out the columns in Table 2.4.

Table 2.4. Your Turn: Instructional Chain

Learning Objective(s)	Activities	Knowledge Processes	Digital Tools	Attributes of Digital Text

Begin with the learning objective. Then, list briefly each activity focusing on what candidates are doing. For example:

- Read textbook
- Watch video
- Complete quiz
- Reflect on lesson plan

Once the activities are listed, think about each and label them as one of the four knowledge processes (i.e., experiencing, conceptualizing, analyzing, applying). Now, think about if and how you can modify the activity to use a digital tool. This may not be possible, which is fine because some instruction, even in online courses, combines digital and non-digital tools. If you are able to conceptualize how a digital tool would benefit candidate learning, list the attributes of digital text you would leverage in the activities (i.e., multimodality, malleability, nonlinearity, interactivity, collaboration). Once finished, review the document and determine if there are changes you would make to the activities now that technology is integrated.

SUMMARY

The purpose of this chapter is to provide a concrete framework from which to structure your online course design. What I find especially appealing is that the pedagogy of multiliteracies considers approaches to teaching in tandem with attributes of digital text. The combination of these elements highlights the uniqueness of the learning space and serves as a reminder of the vastness of the online university classroom.

The next section of this book, along with the companion website, introduces a variety of evidence-based practices and examples of designing instruction that reflect the different activity types discussed in this module. It also provides opportunities to construct your own instructional chains. Be sure to bookmark this chapter so you can refer to its ideas and your application of them for intentional incorporation of the four knowledge processes, considerations of digital and non-digital activities, and reconceptualization of face-to-face instruction to digital delivery.

Part II

DEVELOPING EVIDENCE-BASED ONLINE INSTRUCTION

CHAPTER 3

Think Alouds

Stephen, a middle school science major, was asked to describe his biggest challenge during student teaching:

> It was definitely putting what my professors taught me in class into action in my field placement. Even though I thought I knew what I was doing, it was like I was missing a step between knowing what to do and then actually doing it.

EVIDENCE-BASED PRACTICE: THINK ALOUDS

The gap that Stephen refers to above is a common challenge I hear from teacher education candidates. Although our goal is for them to apply the theoretical and practical applications we teach to diverse educational settings, the realities of K–12 schools can easily hinder teachers' best-developed plans. To scaffold candidates' transition to real-time teaching, it is useful to provide multiple opportunities where they can reflect deeply on course content and translate it into practice. One way to do this is with *think alouds*, the practice of verbalizing one's process of meaning-making while engaging in a cognitive task (Pressley & Afflerbach, 1995).

Researchers have studied think aloud instruction in preschool (Dorl, 2007), elementary school (Migyanka, Policastro, & Lui, 2005), middle and high school (Coiro, 2011; Lapp, Fisher, & Grant, 2008), and college (Ebner & Ehri, 2013). Studies have examined the practice with varied text formats (narrative [Dymock, 2007], informational [Coiro & Dobler, 2007], and digital [Karchmer-Klein & Shinas, 2019]) and in different content areas (math [Banse, Palacios, Merritt, & Rimm-Kaufman, 2017], science [Ortleib & Norris, 2012], and literacy [Karchmer-Klein, 2007]). Moreover, researchers have explored think alouds with diverse learners, including English Language Learners (McKeown & Gentilucci, 2007) and students with reading difficulties (Smith, 2006). Overall, findings from these studies suggest think aloud instruction can positively impact learning.

DIGITAL THINK ALOUDS

Think alouds can be relatively easy to integrate into online coursework given the affordances associated with digital tools (see Table 3.1. for a selection of tools for digital think alouds). Audio and video capabilities, for instance, permit candidates to show their knowledge rather than articulate understandings solely through written language. As a result, think alouds can scaffold candidates' transition from knowing what to do to doing it.

Benefits of Digital Think Alouds

Candidate Think Alouds. There are several benefits to candidates creating digital think alouds (White, 2016). One is repeated practice. Since composing a think aloud takes preparation, it can take several attempts to record the final version. Candidates, in turn, strengthen their skills each time they go through the process. Another benefit is the improvement of communication skills. Most digital tools allow for interactivity and collaboration with classmates or a broader audience. Thus, candidates should consider who they are communicating with when selecting words, images, and sounds used to present content. Third, digital think alouds require the selection of tools that enable cognitive tasks to be documented. The process of creating them allocates time to learn about the affordances and constraints of a wide range of digital tools. Additionally, think alouds can be used as formative assessments. This is especially helpful in online classes where it can be difficult for instructors to pinpoint the exact skills candidates may need help improving.

Table 3.1. Digital Tools for Think Alouds

Digital Tool	Purpose
QuickTime	Screen Capture
Explain Everything	Screen Capture
Show Me	Screen Capture
Vittle Lite	Screen Capture
Screencastify	Screen Capture
Screen-cast-o-matic	Screen Capture
Camtasia	Screen Capture

Instructor Think Alouds. I have found candidates benefit when I create digital think alouds to share with them. I do this in two ways. First, I create think alouds to model concepts or describe assignment directions. For example, over the years, I have learned the importance of providing explicit directions on how to complete online activities. In addition to writing a list of steps, I record a think aloud of me talking through each step, posing anticipated questions, and providing answers. Viewing these think alouds allows candidates to monitor their understanding of the topic or assignment, and, if needed, watch the recorded think aloud repeatedly until it makes sense.

I also utilize think alouds to provide feedback to candidates on their classwork. For example, I use the SpeedGrader tool in Canvas when evaluating writing assignments. This tool displays my scoring rubric in addition to the candidates' submissions. Using a screen capture tool (e.g., QuickTime), I record a think aloud of my grading process. I explain the markups I make as I use highlighting tools and provide context for questions I pose using the commenting tool. Once the digital file is completed, I attach it to the assignment in Canvas. This provides the candidate with personalized feedback in addition to the rubric evaluation. An example of this type of think aloud can be found on the companion website: improvingonlineteachered.com.

Designing Digital Think Aloud Instruction

> As a student watching a think aloud, I appreciate the opportunity to have my instructor's thinking made visible. I can follow along easily and make connections between what they see or are doing on their screen and their thought process in the moment. As the creator, I feel the same way—I am better able to explain my thinking by showing what I am doing along the way.
>
> —Maureen McDonald, EdD Candidate

Screen capture tools record the computer or tablet screen as well as audio, and sometimes video, of the presenter, as users complete a task, making them a great online companion to the practice of think alouds. As shown in Table 3.1., there are many screen capture tools for different operating systems. iPads and some other devices have screen capture tools built into them. Most important, however, is how the tool is used as part of the instructional design, because screen capturing itself does not teach or reinforce a skill.

In the next section I share two examples of instructional design that integrates digital think alouds. Remember, a think aloud is not a lecture. It is an illustration of the cognitive processes one follows as a task is completed.

Digital Think Aloud About Course Content. One type of think aloud I assign requires candidates to illustrate how they experience, conceptualize, analyze, and/or apply a course concept. In other words, candidates show what they know. This type gives an instructor special insight in an online course because it opens a window into candidates' knowledge and can be used as an informal assessment. It also builds community among classmates, as it is a method of sharing candidate voices. There are many ways to design this type of think aloud lesson.

I teach a course called *Foundations of Literacy Instruction* for candidates interested in switching careers and becoming teachers. It can best be described as introductory because it provides an overview of literacy skills and theories. A different topic is unpacked each week through a variety of activities.

The first time I taught the class, I recognized the importance of monitoring candidates' comprehension weekly. Not only was the content new to them, but so was the online delivery. Given this combination, I decided to assign weekly digital think alouds. I designed an activity that would require them to follow the same process of creating a think aloud each week, but with different content. This would make it easier to accomplish as they became more adept with the technology.

Figure 3.1 presents the think aloud portion of a larger module on phonemic awareness (PA), the ability to manipulate sounds orally. Before the think aloud can take place, candidates need to build a basic understanding of PA skills and components of effective instruction. They engage in a combination of activities that require them to experience PA, such as reading research on the topic, and watching video cases of classroom implementation. Once candidates successfully pass a quiz that assesses their knowledge of PA, they move on to analyzing a variety of instructional practices and assessments. Not until this foundational knowledge has been built do I invite candidates to apply their understanding of PA to the activities that include a think aloud.

When assigning a grade to this type of think aloud, it is important to focus on the accuracy of the content, not the aesthetics of the presentation. For example, does the definition of the concept match the definition taught in class? Are class readings used to support statements? With that said, I do not always grade think alouds. It goes back to my purpose for assigning them. If I know candidates are struggling with a concept, I use

Figure 3.1. Think Aloud About Course Content

Learning Objective:

- Demonstrate understanding of effective phonemic awareness instruction by analyzing a lesson.

ILA Standards for the Preparation of Literacy Professionals 2017:

- ILA 2.1: Candidates demonstrate the ability to critically examine pre-K/primary literacy curricula and select high-quality literary, multimedia, and informational texts to provide a coherent, integrated, and motivating literacy program.

ISTE Standards for Teachers:

- Design or adapt relevant learning experiences that incorporate digital tools and resources to promote student learning and creativity.

Activities:

- Experience
  - » Choose a website or computer application that is designed to provide practice of phonemic awareness skills.
  - » Familiarize yourself with the website/app and participate in the activities. *Keep in mind that not all activities will be good models for phonemic awareness instruction.*
- Analyze
  - » Choose one activity to analyze closely.
  - » Reflect deeply upon the activity. Consider whether or not it is a good model of a phonemic awareness activity and whether or not you would use it in the classroom with children.
  - » Take notes on the following:
    - ✓ Definition of phonemic awareness
    - ✓ Description of the activity
    - ✓ Three examples of how the activity does or does not reinforce phonemic awareness with direct references to class readings
- Apply
  - » Create a screen capture of your reflection using the notes you took during analysis. As you record your computer screen, think aloud as you show us the activity as you describe your analysis.
  - » Paste the screen capture link in the class discussion board for your classmates and instructor to view.
- Analyze
  - » Review a classmate's think aloud and post on the discussion board responses to the following:
    - ✓ Would you add anything to the definition of PA?
    - ✓ Do you agree or disagree with your classmate's analysis of the activity and rationale?

Digital Tools:

- Screen Capture Tool
- LMS Discussion Board

the information to modify my instruction to strengthen the areas in need of improvement. If candidates have illustrated understanding of the concepts through other activities, I may assign a graded think aloud to use as an assessment of a larger unit of study.

Digital Think Aloud for the Professional Setting. The second type of think aloud I assign is designed to strengthen candidates' communication skills, provide practice implementing the skill or strategy in their own professional settings, and/or teach others how to integrate the skill or strategy in their own instruction. Elements such as attention to audience, word choice, clarity of points, and cohesiveness of message are prioritized. Additionally, professionalism is assessed by evaluating the speaker's tone and preparedness as well as the overall quality of the video. Figure 3.2 presents an example lesson of this type of think aloud, and an example of a candidate's think aloud can be found on the companion website: improvingonlineteachered.com.

If used regularly in teacher education, this type of think aloud provides the scaffolding discussed earlier in the chapter that would help candidates like Stephen transfer what is learned in the university classroom to real-time teaching.

YOUR TURN

In this chapter you learned different approaches to integrating digital think alouds into online teaching. This section offers an opportunity to design a series of activities that require candidates to create a think aloud. Use Table 3.2 to scaffold your design. A few reminders:

- Identify your learning objective(s). When selecting these, decide if you want the think aloud to be about course content or a method of practicing for use in the candidates' professional settings.
- Brainstorm activities candidates need to complete before and after they create a think aloud in order to meet the learning objectives.
- Identify the type(s) of knowledge processes associated with each activity.
- Determine if there are additional activities you could include to challenge candidates in different ways.
- Brainstorm digital tools that could be integrated into the activities. For example, do you want candidates to screen capture their think aloud or videotape themselves teaching a lesson? If

Figure 3.2. Think Aloud for the Professional Setting

Learning Objective:

- Create a think aloud to be used as a model to teach a concept in your professional setting.
- Analyze a think aloud to identify strengths and areas in need of improvement to clearly articulate processes presented.

ISTE Standards for Teachers:

- Design or adapt relevant learning experiences that incorporate digital tools and resources to promote student learning and creativity.

Activities:

- Experience
  - » Read assigned articles on digital think alouds
  - » Watch video: *5 Ways to Use Screencasts as a Teacher* by Ave Maria Press: www.youtube.com/watch?v=vK1MLWMbDOI
- Conceptualize and Analyze
  - » Choose a lesson or topic in any content area you currently teach.
  - » Choose a component of the lesson that requires a process to be followed. For example:
    - ✓ Mathematical computation
    - ✓ Identification of main idea of a passage
    - ✓ Scientific hypothesis
  - » Analyze the process and draft a list of steps that need to be taken to complete it.
- Apply
  - » Using the materials from the lesson and a screen capture tool, create a think aloud of the process.
  - » Post link to the think aloud in the LMS Discussion Board.
- Analyze
  - » Review a classmate's think aloud and analyze the steps followed. Determine if the points are well articulated with appropriate word choice, language, and tone, speaker is prepared, and all necessary steps were incorporated.
  - » Provide written feedback to your classmate about the think aloud on the LMS Discussion Board.

Digital Tools:

- Screen Capture Tool
- LMS Discussion Board

so, will you require they use a particular tool or provide a menu of options? Also, consider the tools' affordances in light of the activities you are assigning.

SUMMARY

This chapter introduced the idea of digital think alouds as a practice that can be seamlessly integrated into online courses. It is also a particularly useful evidence-based practice because it is one most teacher education candidates will use in their own professional settings, whether it be with K–12 students or colleagues through professional development opportunities.

Table 3.2. Your Turn: Think Alouds

Learning Objective(s)	Activities	Knowledge Processes	Digital Tools	Attributes of Digital Text

CHAPTER 4

Case-Based Instruction

As with any learning space, online classes should provide
opportunities to engage with colleagues around course content.
By integrating case-based instruction, I aim to encourage active
engagement through discussions of issues and problems presented,
so teacher participants have opportunities to develop connections
between theory and practice.

—Amber Warren, PhD, Assistant Professor

In his 1985 presidential address to the American Education Research
Association, Lee Shulman encouraged the use of case-based instruction
(CBI) in teacher education for the purpose of developing knowledge
of teaching and reflection on practice. Over the years, as illustrated by
Amber's remarks above, CBI has become more widely used to teach
concepts and problem-solving strategies to preservice and practicing educators (e.g. Dietz & Davis, 2009; Luo, Koszalka, Arnone, & Choi, 2018).

EVIDENCE-BASED PRACTICE: CASE-BASED INSTRUCTION

CBI is a pedagogical approach that immerses candidates in situations
they may encounter in their future professional practice. The activities
require classmates to work independently and collectively to examine,
analyze, and reflect upon actual or hypothetical discipline-specific scenarios (Ertmer & Koehler, 2018). Research indicates CBI is more useful for
teaching candidates to transfer theory to practice than are traditional texts
or teaching techniques (Shulman, 1986). Well-designed scenarios require
sophisticated and strategic analysis, which in turn build the skills necessary to solve complex problems (Choi & Lee, 2009). These scenarios also
place candidates in professional contexts where they apply the types of
situational knowledge held by experienced educators. Additionally, the
collaborative and interactive nature of CBI improves communication skills

as candidates must effectively articulate opinions, debate differences, and resolve misconceptions.

Selecting Case Studies

Cases are at the center of CBI and should be chosen carefully. Clear course objectives should be identified first so it can be determined whether the cases selected will lead to the intended learning goals.

One approach to selecting CBI is to use cases authored by publishers or other educators. These may be accessible in textbooks or online. However, it is difficult to find cases written by others that perfectly align to your specific course objectives. Therefore, a second approach is for instructors to write their own cases with direct connections between case content and learning objectives. Another approach is to require candidates to compose cases about their own teaching. This provides concrete opportunities for learners to apply theory to relatable professional contexts. Moreover, it may motivate candidates to reflect more deeply on their own teaching.

A word of caution. Cases are not easy to write for instructors or students. Situations must be presented so that candidates can extrapolate details and analyze them in ways that meet learning objectives. To scaffold the process of case writing, Ertmer and Russell (1995) suggest brainstorming the following questions:

- What's the big idea?
- What's the story?
- Who are the characters?
- What's the dilemma?

Once these questions are answered, they recommend using the following writing format:

1. Describe the overall goal
2. Connect directly to learning objectives
3. Present scenario
4. Share relevant evidence
5. Identify questions for class discussion

Hammerness, Darling-Hammond, and Shulman (2002) recommend scaffolding the case writing experience even more when candidates compose them. They suggest a multistep process that begins with applying theory to case studies written by other educators. Candidates unpack these by analyzing the elements that connect to the theory and practices learned in class. Next, candidates outline and draft their own case studies based upon their teaching situation, using a rubric like the one shown in Table 4.1 to guide their writing. Instructors create the initial rubric with appropriate evaluative elements, and candidates are invited to modify it once they better understand the characteristics of good case studies and know the facts they need for the content area.

Hammerness et al. (2002) also suggest case writing be followed by peer review, where teacher candidates work with partners to closely examine each other's cases. Partners apply the rubric to their classmate's work and provide feedback. The final step is to engage candidates in small-group feedback sessions, where cases are presented to classmates and discussion ensues.

Designing Case-Based Instruction

The design of a CBI activity is critical to the effectiveness of the pedagogical practice. Instructors must be well versed in the specifics of a case so they can prepare candidates to unpack the details, ensuring information is not missed. Additionally, instructors must think carefully about how best to scaffold thoughtful reflection and discussion of cases. For CBI to be most effective, candidates must first have acquired pedagogical knowledge that will enable them to deeply examine the case. In some cases, instructors may direct candidates with limited foundational knowledge to focus on the specific areas for which they are prepared.

I engage candidates in three types of CBI activities in my online courses. One focuses on *skill application*. After introducing new content, candidates are presented a case that requires them to apply what they learned from class resources to a given situation. There is typically one correct answer so that it is clear to the instructor if candidates understand concepts at the literal level. The second type of activity requires candidates to analyze situations from *multiple points of view*. This requires deep analysis of cases and the ability to see situations from alternative perspectives. *Problem-solving* is a third type of CBI. Perhaps the most complex, these activities require candidates to integrate theoretical and practical knowledge with content presented in the given situation to analyze problems and identify potential solutions.

Table 4.1. Case Writing Rubric

Elements	Meets Expectations	Developing	Does Not Meet Expectations
Purpose	Narrative identifies a clear educational purpose.	Narrative identifies a general educational purpose but would benefit from a narrower focus.	Narrative does not identify a purpose.
Context • Stakeholders (e.g., teachers, students, administrators) • School • Community	Narrative provides details about all aspects of educational context including descriptions of stakeholders as individuals and who they are as a group (if working with more than one).	Narrative provides general information related to the educational context. Stakeholders are described as a group with little or no detail about who they are as individuals.	Narrative is brief with little to no information about educational context and/or stakeholders.
Scenario	Narrative provides a clear description of scenario to be analyzed including details such as stakeholders' reactions and/or dialogue among and between them.	Narrative provides a description of scenario with some detail but would benefit from more details to provide reader with more information to analyze.	Narrative provides a brief description of scenario with little to no detail.
Discussion Prompts	Narrative includes prompts directly related to aspects of the scenario to launch discussion among readers.	Narrative includes prompts that may launch general discussions about scenario.	Narrative does not include discussion prompts or prompts do not relate to scenario.

DIGITAL CASE-BASED INSTRUCTION

Online learning environments lend themselves well to CBI. Case evidence can be presented multimodally, using combinations of video, written documents, audio, figures, charts, and tables (see Table 4.2 for a selection of tools for digital CBI). Case discussions can take place between classmates using LMS discussion or video conferencing tools or third-party cloud-based tools. The process of reflection, a critical step in CBI, can take place with written language or through multimodal presentations. Overall, CBI can be as simple or complex as you want it depending upon the learning objectives of the lesson and your willingness to leverage the attributes of digital tools.

In the remainder of this chapter, I share examples of CBI taken from courses I've designed for undergraduate and graduate programs in literacy and teacher leadership. I also provide lessons I learned throughout the years as I designed CBI as well as tips about using video for case studies. Keep in mind that the cases are just one component of the instruction. Again, to prepare candidates to participate in CBI, they must first experience content that builds foundational knowledge of the topic which they can later conceptualize, analyze, and apply to the cases.

Skill Application

I often create my own cases when I want to use CBI for skill application. I find this approach allows me to present scenarios that match most closely to my primary learning goal, which is to strengthen content knowledge. I suggest keeping these cases relatively simple with few

Table 4.2. Digital Tools for Case-Based Instruction

Digital Tool	Purpose
VoiceThread	Case Presentation
Quicktime	Screencapture/Video Creation
Vialogues	Time-Stamp Video
GoReact	Time-Stamp Video
TurboNote	Time-Stamp Video
Camtasia	Time-Stamp Video
Twitter	Backchanneling
Question Cookie	Backchanneling
GarageBand	Podcasting
Audacity	Podcasting

distractors. This design allows candidates to focus on particular content and helps the instructor quickly assess whether or not skills have been mastered.

The easiest way to incorporate a case for skill application is to post a short scenario in your LMS discussion board and ask pointed questions that prompt candidates to identify specific content. For example, in a course titled *Coaching Teachers,* this case teaches the important skill of paraphrasing through a series of activities.

1. **Experience:** In a video-recorded lecture, I introduce the characteristics of paraphrasing and why the skill is important when coaching. I provide multiple examples.
2. **Experience:** Candidates read an online article on paraphrasing.
3. **Conceptualize:** Candidates watch a video of a coaching meeting where a coach paraphrases as she works with a teacher. The video is uploaded to Vialogues where I have time-stamped examples of the characteristics of paraphrasing as a model for candidates. Candidates are directed to compare content learned about paraphrasing to my model.
4. **Apply:** Candidates read three scenarios that reflect a coach–teacher conversation, identify the type of scaffolded paraphrasing that is represented in each, and provide a justification.
5. **Analyze:** Candidates read a group member's response, analyze justification, and provide feedback that connects directly back to course content in the form of questions, affirmations, or disagreements.

Figure 4.1 presents an example of this type of case.

Since these activities take place online, I sometimes incorporate different digital tools so that I am simultaneously bolstering candidates' technology skills. VoiceThread offers candidates choice in the modality they use to respond. In the introductory course, *Understanding Teacher Leadership,* candidates learn about different leadership styles. Once they've built sufficient foundational knowledge through readings and video lectures, I present a series of scenarios in VoiceThread, which candidates respond to using audio or video. Since the tool affords them the opportunity to interact with classmates, they are also asked to analyze their classmates' views of the scenarios and compare their responses. Directions given to the candidates and a scenario are presented in Figure 4.2.

Figure 4.1. Example of Skill Application Case Activity

Directions:

Read the teacher statement below and respond as a coach by writing a paraphrased statement that *acknowledges and/or clarifies.* State your response in your discussion post along with a justification of why it is appropriate by connecting it to the definitions of paraphrasing presented in class. Be explicit so your justification is clear.

Teacher Statement:

"The student doesn't come to school several times a week. How will it impact his learning and how can I be held responsible?"

Candidate Response:

"You're feeling frustrated that this student is missing your lessons regularly."

The definition of acknowledging and clarifying a teacher statement is "Restate the essence of what was said." Essentially this teacher is frustrated that the student is not attending school and therefore is missing the lessons that she is likely planning very hard for. The teacher is outwardly expressing that they are feeling discouraged and frustrated by the student's absences because it is going to affect the grade and the student is missing so much.

Classmate Response:

For Question 2, do you think your paraphrasing would make more of an impact if you added something about the student not learning the work, not being proficient in the standards, or meeting the grade level goals? You did a good job mentioning that the teacher is frustrated that the student is missing her lessons, but I think the teacher needs to know that the coach realizes that the teacher is frustrated because the student may not reach the grade level goals. Possibly another way you could paraphrase would be: "You're feeling frustrated that this student is missing your lessons regularly and you are concerned that he/she may not reach the grade level standard goals."

Figure 4.2. Directions and Scenario for VoiceThread Skill Application Case

Guidelines

Read a series of scenarios. Choose two to respond to on the appropriate VoiceThread slides. Afterward, listen to your classmates' posts to compare your responses.

Scenario

Mr. Cummings is a brand new 10th-grade science teacher. He quickly becomes a student favorite and soon invites students to join his personal Instagram account and Facebook page. Once you learn about this, as his assigned mentor, you schedule a meeting with him to discuss the matter and tell him to make his social media accounts private and block all students who have access. In your video response, address the following:

1. Which leadership style is reflected in the scenario?
2. Is it the approach you would choose, or would a different style be more effective? Explain your answer.

Alternative Perspectives

Encouraging teacher education candidates to consider alternative per-spectives can be beneficial for many reasons. It can foster open-mind-edness, leading to a wider discourse on issues that matter in their educational setting. It can help candidates build sensitivity and patience with students and colleagues in the workplace. Additionally, under-standing alternative perspectives on pressing issues can strengthen com-munication skills so candidates are better able to articulate their own views.

My go-to lesson design for this type of CBI is what I call *What in the World?* Like the television show *Law & Order*, I rip stories from the headlines of professional educational publications and podcasts like *Educational Leadership, Conversations US,* or *NPREd,* and share them as case studies that need to be unpacked and analyzed from different per-spectives. I choose provocative cases without right or wrong answers with the goal of precipitating debate. The activity begins with an intro-duction followed by two to four sources on the topic presented from different perspectives. Topics have included the national teacher short-age, parent outrage over standardized testing, and educators' mishaps with social media. After candidates have time to process the cases in-dependently, they are assigned or invited to choose a perspective from which to respond to the situation. This step shifts thinking from their own opinion to that of another stakeholder. To conclude, candidates in-teract with classmates through the discussion board or other technology tool to discuss and argue points further.

Figure 4.3 presents an example of a *What in the World* case on the topic of the Atlanta school system cheating scandal. I have incorporated this case several times. It always starts spirited discussions, perhaps because the majority of candidates are practicing teachers who are all too familiar with the demands of state testing.

Each semester I also assign one opportunity for candidates to create a *What in the World* case for their classmates to analyze and discuss. This immerses them in a search for contemporary issues that are taking place outside of their professional settings or related to situations they deal with at their own locations. One candidate, a high school physics teacher, shared newspaper articles on the topic of assessment retakes, something his school was working through at the time. Other topics have included student attendance, student equity, mindfulness in elementary schools, and corporal punishment in schools.

Figure 4.3. Example of *What in the World?* Case Study

Learning Objective:

- Analyze a case study from alternative perspectives and apply leadership skills to make recommendations for change.

Teacher Leader Model Standards:

- Domain III: Promoting Professional Learning for Continuous Improvement
- Domain VI: Improving Outreach and Collaboration with Families and Community

ISTE Standards for Teachers:

- Engage in professional growth and leadership

Activities:

- Experience
  - » Candidates watch *PBS Newshour* clip about the Atlanta school system's cheating scandal.
- Analyze
  - » Candidates analyze facts from the video clip and identify evident leadership failures.
  - » Candidates re-analyze the case from the position of a different stakeholder than their current professional position: for example, principal, student, teacher, parent, or administrator.
- Apply
  - » From the alternate point of view, candidates post their analysis of the situation in the discussion board, outline the stakeholder's responsibility, and explain if and how the response could have been different.
  - » Candidates read posts written from the same perspective and pose questions, affirm, or disagree with the statements.

Digital Tools:

  - » Video: *Learning Matters: Cheating in Atlanta*: www.youtube.com/watch?v=C9ZHk-WDTN0
  - » LMS discussion board

Problem Solving

When different types of cases are integrated into instruction, candidates experience a wide range of potential situations, and instructors prepare them to flexibly respond to problems they encounter in their professional settings. Below I share examples of problem-solving case studies utilizing different digital tools and approaches.

Podcasts and Backchanneling. I try to expose teacher education candidates to as many digital tools as possible, so they build their technology skills while they acquire content knowledge. Combining *podcasts* with *backchanneling* is a fruitful approach to engaging candidates in problem-solving cases. The podcasts are audio clips of education-related scenarios. Backchanneling is a method of holding conversations concurrent to activities taking place. In this type of CBI activity, candidates respond to, query, and summarize cases using a backchanneling tool (e.g., Twitter, Question Cookie) as they listen to a case study podcast. They can follow the stream of thought on the backchanneling tool before, during, and after they complete the case.

I first got this idea when I came across Joe Mazza's work with the University of Pennsylvania's Mid-Career Innovations Lab (soundcloud.com/mcilab), affiliated with Penn's Mid-Career Doctoral Program in Educational Leadership. Mazza and colleagues produced the BackchannelEDU "a scenario-based podcast based on connecting research to practice across the educational space and involve real roles, real leadership scenarios complete with real voices from the field, cutting across race, gender, class, ethnicity and sexuality." Free to anyone with the link, the purpose of the BackchannelEDU was to put listeners in a leadership role as they listen to the facts of a case and then pose questions, share solutions, or suggest additional resources on Twitter using a class hashtag. By including the hashtag, all responses to the scenario could be compiled on the same Twitter feed and easily accessed and reviewed.

This CBI activity requires several steps. Candidates must have a Twitter account. They must also understand how to use the tool. Although this may seem obvious, in my experience, Twitter is not intuitive and can be difficult to master. Additionally, I like to curate my candidates' tweets using my own private course Twitter account, so I create a new one each semester and share it with the class.

I have used the BackchannelEDU scenarios along with backchanneling in the online course, *Fostering Technology-Based Collaborations,* a requirement of a MEd in Teacher Leadership degree. Figure 4.4 presents the activities that make up this type of CBI using the scenario Tap Out (soundcloud.com/mcilab/s2-episode-02-tap-out-bedu0202). In this scenario, the school principal explains a situation where three students decide to see "what it was like to put each other into submission until they passed out." The principal outlines several issues he is confronting and asks leaders to problem-solve appropriate consequences since the incident took place on school grounds and other students are aware of what happened because it was videotaped. Figure 4.5 is an example of a candidate's tweet suggesting a possible solution.

Figure 4.4. Example of a Podcast/Backchanneling Case

Learning Objective:

- Analyze a case study and apply leadership skills to provide support to other leaders.
- Examine a range of digital tools and use them to collaborate with others.
- Analyze use of social media in professional development

Teacher Leader Model Standards:

- Domain III: Promoting Professional Learning for Continuous Improvement
- Domain VI: Improving Outreach and Collaboration with Families and Community

ISTE Standards for Teachers:

- Engage in professional growth and leadership

Activities:

- Experience
  - » Candidates read articles about Twitter and its use in education.
  - » Candidates watch a video tutorial on setting up a Twitter account.
- Conceptualize
  - » Candidates practice using Twitter by participating in at least two chats on an education-related topic of their choice.
- Experience
  - » Candidates read articles on backchanneling and its use in education.
- Experience
  - » Candidates read articles on podcasting.
- Conceptualize
  - » Candidates listen to at least three education-related podcasts and Tweet a link to their favorite one.
- Experience, Analyze, Apply
  - » Candidates listen to the Tap Out podcast by Penn's Mid-Career Innovations Lab: https://soundcloud.com/mcilab/s2-episode-02-tap-out-bedu0202
  - » Candidates reflect on the questions posed on the podcast and post questions, summaries, and or other statements on Twitter including the course hashtag.
- Analyze
  - » Candidates analyze the experience of completing the podcast/backchanneling case by posting a reflection on the class discussion board.

Digital Tools:

- Podcast
- Twitter
- LMS discussion board

Figure 4.5. Candidate's Tweet

@educ777sp17 As a TL, I would
plan a school-wide assembly to
educate students on dangers of
tap out & invite community
members (police etc)

Since this case is assigned in a course about using technology in leadership, I extend the activities beyond case analysis to include reflection on the experience of using podcasting and backchanneling for professional development. The majority of reflections tend to be positive, like those listed below:

- I wasn't sure what to expect but was pleasantly surprised when I started listening and realized that it was a scenario that we were being asked for input on from the administrator. It caught and maintained my interest much more than reading a bunch of scenarios from a powerpoint or presentation would.
- I felt it was challenging, frustrating, exciting and a learning journey. For such a "short and simple" activity (listen to a podcast and Tweet a response), it actually had so many intricate layers that required a lot of thought and self-reflection.
- This type of professional development activity was one of the first that truly held my interest as a student, teacher and aspiring teacher leader. I often find the PD opportunities in my environment to be not applicable to my particular setting, or non-continual.

Yet not all candidates favor this approach. The primary challenge has to do with using Twitter as the backchanneling tool. When I first implemented this lesson in my class, Twitter limited tweets to 140 characters. Candidates found this allotment too constraining to share thoughtful responses to the case. Fewer candidates mention character limits as a constraint once Twitter increased it to 280. In fact, several candidates have remarked that the character limit challenges them to be succinct in their responses to the activity. As one student explained,

The fact that Twitter only uses 280 characters forces the educator to get to the point quickly and allows for others to read through the many solutions more efficiently. Getting bogged down in too many details or lengthy explanations is not an option when responding with this backchanneling tool.

Of course, Twitter is not the only option for this type of activity. There are other backchannel options including Facebook, Edmodo, Question Cookie, or AnswerGarden. I recommend trying different ones to see which best meets your learning objectives and technology preference.

Case Writing and Situated Learning. When my colleagues and I designed our graduate online program in literacy, we agreed *situated learning* would be a hallmark of all coursework. This was partly due to our collective pedagogical beliefs about learning, but also because the state department of education required candidates to apply assessment and instructional literacy practices in authentic educational contexts. We made it essential for candidates to have access to a professional setting where they could implement and reflect upon practices we taught them. Because of this programmatic decision, the integration of CBI has been seamless because (1) we know candidates are situated in settings where they can work directly with students, colleagues, or other stakeholders throughout the semester and (2) we can be sure they will experience problems or concerns they can draw upon for case writing.

Supervised Reading Clinic is a six-credit required course in the MEd in Literacy program. During the semester, candidates tutor a student identified as having difficulties in reading. Candidates are expected to apply the knowledge learned in earlier literacy courses to design and implement appropriate instruction for their student. Additionally, candidates work collaboratively to brainstorm and problem-solve questions and concerns.

When I taught in a traditional brick-and-mortar, face-to-face program, I would hold the clinic at a local elementary school during the summer. Class would meet Monday through Friday for 4 hours a day for 5 weeks. A portion of each session would consist of group activities and one-on-one tutoring with the K–12 students. After tutoring, students would leave and the remaining time would be focused on the candidates writing and discussing case studies which included assessment data, reflection on daily instruction, and questions about how to proceed.

Now that the clinic is held fully online, I rely heavily on case writing. The online delivery enables candidates to leverage technological affordances to share their cases with the instructor and classmates using different presentation formats and feedback tools. Figure 4.6 shows an example of a problem-solving case writing assignment, including step-by-step directions to provide readers with a concrete example and a rubric to evaluate candidate work.

The ILA *Standards for the Preparation of Literacy Professionals 2017* (2018), Reading/Literacy Specialist, require candidates to illustrate their ability to select, administer, and accurately analyze assessment data as well as present their findings to different stakeholders. Formerly, this standard was met when candidates composed a written report, which was then shared with parents and classroom teachers. For the online course, I decided to leverage multimodality and instead have the students create digital presentations where they orally reported their findings and used visual representations (e.g., data tables) to justify their decisionmaking. Candidates are now challenged to curate their data and accurately present the details of their cases using multiple modes of communication.

The rubric presented in Table 4.3 was used to evaluate the assignment above. It was revised several times with the whole class to include candidates' views of what was important to share in their cases.

Figure 4.6. Case Writing: Literacy Assessment

Learning Objective:

- Illustrate accurate analysis of literacy assessment data.
- Design and present a case to a stakeholder illustrating understanding of assessment data and justification for instructional decisionmaking.
- Utilize digital tools to professionally present a case.

ILA Standards for the Preparation of Literacy Professionals 2017:

- ILA 3.2: Candidates collaborate with colleagues to administer, interpret, and use data for decision making about student assessment, instruction, intervention, and evaluation for individual and groups of students.

ISTE Standards for Teachers:

- Use assessment data to guide progress and communicate with students, parents and education stakeholders to build student self-direction.

Activities:

- Analyze
  - » Collect data from at least two literacy assessments previously administered to your student.
  - » Research any assessments you are unfamiliar with by reviewing manuals and other test information.
  - » Analyze the assessment data looking for common strengths and weaknesses and areas to target for instruction.
- Apply
  - » Choose a stakeholder to whom you will present the case analysis of your student's literacy assessment results. Stakeholders could be parents, students, teachers, specialists, or administrators.
  - » Using the rubric to guide the development of your case, create a VoiceThread case presentation where you will:
    - ✓ Introduce case.
    - ✓ Provide context for case.
    - ✓ Communicate the results of two previous assessments administered to your student. Be sure to state the assessment name, its purpose, and any other details such as how it is administered (e.g., individual, computer-based). Include visual representations of student data.
    - ✓ Advocate for an appropriate plan of action for administering additional assessments to identify primary and secondary literacy skills in need of improvement.
    - ✓ Provide justification for administering additional assessments.
  - » Post link to your case presentation in the discussion box below. Make sure others can access it.
  - » Post two prompts to launch discussion among classmates about potential problems related to instructional decisions.
- Analyze and Apply
  - » Review a group member's assessment case. Comment on each slide with feedback in the form of questions, statements, or answers in response to the discussion prompts.

Digital Tools:

- PowerPoint or Keynote
- VoiceThread
- LMS Discussion Board

Table 4.3. Case Writing Rubric for Literacy Assessment Presentation

Elements	Meets Expectations	Developing	Does Not Meet Expectations
Purpose of Case	Candidate clearly articulates the purpose of the case.	Candidate describes case in broad terms without a clear direction for reader to contextualize its purpose.	Candidate does not state the purpose of the case.
Professional Context	Community and school contexts are described. Student is described including age, ethnicity, language spoken at home, diverse needs, other factors (e.g., reading behaviors at home)	Broad description of setting. More detail would provide a clearer illustration of the content.	Few, if any, descriptors of setting are provided.
Assessments	The purpose of each assessment is accurate. The scoring procedures for the assessments are accurate.	The purpose of each assessment and the scoring procedures are mostly accurate. Some of the major aspects of the assessment are not mentioned (e.g., adaptive computer test).	It is not clear if the candidate understands the purpose of the assessments and/or scoring procedures.
Assessment Data	Assessment data are presented using visual representations and analyzed correctly by the candidate.	Assessment data are presented. The visual representations are unclear and/or analyses are brief. More detail would be beneficial to illustrate understanding of assessment results.	Assessment data are presented but visual representations and/or analyses are incorrect.
Instructional Decisions	Candidate explains how data from student should be used to make at least two instructional decisions about literacy instruction.	Candidate explains how data from student should be used to make instructional decisions about literacy instruction but rationale is weak and could be stronger.	Instructional decisions do not reflect data results.
Case Prompts	Candidate includes at least two well-written prompts in the case that will facilitate discussion among classmates about anticipated problems related to instructional decisions.	Candidate includes prompts in the case to facilitate discussion among classmates about instructional decisions. Prompts are general or confusing and would benefit from revision.	Candidate includes prompts that are not relevant to the information provided in the case.

CHOOSING AND USING VIDEO FOR CASE-BASED INSTRUCTION

When designing activities to facilitate thoughtful analysis of cases, I rely quite a bit on video. Research has found this mode to be a useful scaffold for candidates as they learn to connect theory to practice (Mosley Wetzel, Maloch, Hoffman, Taylor, Vlach, & Greeter, 2015).

With the variety of digital portals available on the Internet, such as YouTube, TeacherTube, and Teaching Channel, instructors can easily find videos related to course content. Some are shared by experts in the field while others are created by practitioners. Of course, it is important to determine the appropriateness of the video before using it in class. Instructors should ask:

- Who is the developer?
- What is the quality?
- What are the practices illustrated and do they match the learning objectives?

I think it is acceptable to use video cases that illustrate what *not* to do in the classroom. I've done this several times when I want to assess candidates' ability to discern between effective and poor implementation of teaching practices.

Interactions about video cases can take place in an LMS or a cloud-based tool. When designing video CBI, I like to use time-stamp digital applications, which allow users to type comments as they watch a video. The notes are then time-stamped onto the video and can be read by others as they follow the case, adding to the community of collaborative learning.

Time-Stamped Video

I use time-stamp video tools in different ways. One is to model content for candidates. For example, I described a lesson earlier in this chapter that taught candidates about paraphrasing. After presenting a video lecture to introduce them to the skill, they watched a video I inserted into Vialogues, a free cloud-based time-stamp tool created by a team at EdLab at Teachers College Columbia University. The video I inserted was created by Glenda Baker, an instructional coach, and found on YouTube. As candidates watched the coaching conversation, they saw my notes, where I identified instances of paraphrasing, scroll beside the video. This combination of feedback and video provided a concrete model to draw upon once they applied their own knowledge of paraphrasing to cases. This example can be found on the companion website: improvingonlineteachered.com.

Another approach to using time-stamped video is to ask candidates to comment as they watch the video by time-stamping a response to prompts posed by the instructor. Sometimes the prompts are broad, and other times I direct candidates' attention toward particular skills I want to reinforce.

- **Broad:** Post a comment in the video at a point that resonated with you and explain why.
- **Directed:** Post a comment in the video at the point when you learn the main idea of the story. State the evidence directly from the video to support your answer.

A third approach to using time-stamped video is to assign candidates the task of working collaboratively to identify a video that meets a particular learning goal and then annotate it as a group. The *What in the World?* activity described earlier works well with this format. It requires candidates to identify an issue, locate video related to the topic, analyze the content of the video, and work collaboratively to determine where to annotate the video to capture classmates' attention about certain aspects of the case. Additionally, candidates must develop scaffolded prompts to guide their classmates' discussions.

Time-stamped video cases can be used to extend case writing by inviting candidates to work collaboratively to solve problems and explore curriculum innovations in response to cases shared from their professional settings. In most of my courses that integrate CBI, candidates are required to videotape their teaching, coaching, or other field-based activities. Posting these clips in a time-stamp tool and then inviting classmates to help problem-solve particular instances creates an organized space to conduct fluid dialogue between candidates.

Time-stamp tools should be selected based on the type of video case. For example, if I am using a video taken from TeacherTube, I will use a free cloud-based tool such as Vialogues or TurboNote. These videos are freely accessed, so I am not concerned if the tool is password-protected or not. For privacy, I have candidates sign up for free digital tools using either a pseudonym or just their first name and last initial. If candidates are uploading video of their own teaching, it is good practice to use password-protected tools such as your LMS or a third-party tool that your university has purchased such as GoReact.

Safe Practices and Tips for Using Video

All this talk about video requires a conversation about safe practices. Universities must be compliant with the Family Education Rights & Privacy Act (FERPA). As a course instructor, be sure to understand your school's policies about posting candidate work on open-access websites. Below are a few considerations. The list is not exhaustive because it is critical that instructors follow their own school's policies.

- Collect signed permission forms for anyone who will be captured in the video. This includes candidates, students, colleagues, and clinical educators.
- Collect permissions signed by parents for K–12 students who appear.
- Use password-protected digital tools.
- Require candidates to use pseudonyms in their own work and when referring to student work when making videos or other multimodal presentations.

My first few attempts to use video to capture tutoring was messy, mainly because it took a lot of effort to figure out the best way to share video and other data using the LMS. At the time, video clips were too large to upload into the LMS. I worked closely with the IT department to bypass the issue, and we created a password-protected server just for the clinic. Although this was a fix, it was cumbersome. Candidates had to send their videos through the university's cloud-based file-sharing system, and IT support had to upload them onto the server.

Today, inserting video clips is a much easier process. Our LMS can handle larger files, and candidates have become more tech-savvy, especially ones who enroll in fully online programs. In fact, some candidates video their tutoring sessions directly from the computer using the video tool in Canvas.

It is also useful to ask candidates to post portions of their tutoring sessions rather than the full 30–45 minutes. Of course, this reduces the size of the file, but it also focuses viewers' attention on certain aspects of the instruction. To prepare, candidates must review the entire video-recorded lesson and jot down questions and concerns about the instruction or the students' responses. Next, they create a written document that lists two questions or concerns from the original list that they want their classmates to help problem-solve. They also provide a time stamp so classmates can quickly find it in the video. Lastly, they clip the video and upload it to the LMS along with the document and share with the class.

Although current candidates may be tech-savvy, I still find it good practice to provide specific instructions on how to manage video. Currently I use the handout in Figure 4.7. to guide candidates. However, the quick pace of technological advances requires me to continuously update it. I share it here so it can be used as a model, but keep in mind your LMS may require different directions.

Figure 4.7. How to Create and Post a Video Clip

As part of the Supervised Reading Clinic, you are required to video your instruction and post no more than a 3-minute clip on the course discussion board. So how do you do this? Below are two suggestions.

Suggestion #1:

1. Make a video using your iPhone or iPad.
    a. Click on the Camera app.
    b. Make sure it is turned to VIDEO.
    c. Prop device up to capture the conversation.
    d. Open video. Click EDIT. Drag arrows to trim video. Click DONE. Click Trim Original.
2. Send video to your computer to post on Canvas Discussion Board. It will probably open in QuickTime if you are using a Mac.
    a. Airdrop or email it to your computer.
    b. Save to your desktop.
    c. Go to your Discussion Board. Click REPLY. Click the filmstrip icon. Click UPLOAD MEDIA. Click SELECT VIDEO FILE. The video should upload.

Suggestion #2:

1. Make your video using the camera on your laptop. You could use Screencastify (Google Chrome), FaceTime on the Mac, or any other app you choose.
2. Open the video in QuickTime (if you have it on your computer) or another video-editing tool. Click EDIT and click TRIM. You should be able to trim the video to 3 minutes.
3. Send video to your computer to post on Canvas Discussion Board. It will probably open in QuickTime if you are using a Mac.
    a. Airdrop or email it to your computer.
    b. Save to your desktop.
    c. Go to your Discussion Board. Click REPLY. Click the filmstrip icon. Click UPLOAD MEDIA. Click SELECT VIDEO FILE. The video should upload.

YOUR TURN

The section below provides space to practice designing a series of activities that incorporate case-based instruction. I suggest choosing one of the following types:

- Skill application
- Alternative perspectives
- Problem solving

Use Table 4.4 to scaffold your design. A few reminders:

- Identify your learning objective(s). This will dictate the type of CBI you implement.
- Brainstorm activities candidates need to complete before and after they interact with the case.
- Identify the type(s) of knowledge processes associated with each activity.
- Determine if there are additional activities you could include to challenge candidates in different ways.
- Brainstorm digital tools that could be integrated into the activities. Will you require they use a particular tool or will you provide a menu of options? Also, consider the tools' affordances in light of the activities you are assigning.

SUMMARY

This chapter defined case-based instruction and presented different approaches to incorporating different types of CBI activities into online courses. These include skill application, promotion of alternative perspectives, and opportunities to problem-solve. A variety of digital tools was used in the examples and I encourage you to try them out or identify other tools that provide similar affordances. Many online teacher education courses include field experiences, making CBI relatively easy to implement. If your course does not, you can create your own relatable case studies or search through the plethora of resources online.

Table 4.4. Your Turn: Case-Based Instruction

Type of Case:

Learning Objective(s)	Activities	Knowledge Processes	Digital Tools	Attributes of Digital Text

CHAPTER 5

Peer Feedback

Paige and Janae are classmates in the course *Supervised Reading Practicum,* a requirement of the MEd in Literacy program. Both women are tutoring children who have difficulties reading at grade level. As part of the course, they work as a pair to provide feedback to each other prior to tutoring sessions. Below is one of their exchanges:

> *Paige:* Your scope and sequence are very detailed, especially considering you are preparing plans for many different texts. I think the page numbers you provide to be read each day provide good pacing for the length of these lessons. If you find that your student can handle more or less reading, though, would it be easy to adjust these page numbers? I might consider adding different vocabulary for each lesson, rather than the same vocabulary each lesson. You could also spread out the vocabulary you do have, so the child is learning 2–3 terms per day, rather than 5 vocabulary words. If the texts are sectioned to discuss various subtopics, you can choose vocabulary that supports that specific subtopic.
>
> *Janae:* Thanks so much for your feedback! I would definitely adjust the pages if need be. Right now, I have them set up so that the books with the lower Lexile scores we read a few more pages of and the books with higher Lexile scores we read fewer pages of. This is something that could definitely fluctuate. Your ideas about teaching fewer vocabulary words prior to the lesson is a great one. I think this is something that I will work into my lesson plans. It makes sense because he may become overwhelmed.

Paige's review of Janae's lesson included specific references to the instructional steps. She posed questions and offered direct suggestions for modification. This brief excerpt is an example of one type of interactivity to strive for in online courses.

EVIDENCE-BASED PRACTICE: PEER FEEDBACK

Peer feedback in traditional educational settings refers to oral or written exchanges between classmates that further the process of learning for both the provider and receiver (van Popta, Kral, Camp, Martens, & Simons, 2017). These collegial interactions have been found to encourage active learning, strengthen judgment of one's own progress, develop content knowledge, and build social skills (Liu & Carless, 2006; MacArthur, 2016).

There is a robust body of literature reporting positive effects of peer feedback on students' writing skills in elementary school (Philippakos & MacArthur, 2014), middle school (Boscolo & Ascorti (2004), and college (Cho & MacArthur, 2011; Lundstrom & Baker, 2009). *Peer coaching*, another form of peer feedback, takes place when teachers work collaboratively to solve problems and explore curriculum innovations together in their professional setting (Showers & Joyce, 1996). Initially implemented with inservice teachers, it has become more widely used in preservice teacher education (Lu, 2010). Research studying its effects suggest peer coaching promotes reflective teaching by refining teachers' practice and cultivating a community of educators who are dedicated to improving their teaching skills (Soisangwarn & Wongwanich, 2014). Research indicates that peer feedback enhances learning when those providing feedback are specifically taught how to identify markers indicating achievement of learning outcomes (Liu & Carless, 2006; Lu, 2010).

Designing activities that incorporate peer feedback takes planning and scaffolding. Although research suggests it allows for more frequent and reciprocal thought sharing (MacArthur, 2016), there are arguments against using it as an instructional practice. For instance, students may be reluctant to criticize others or accept feedback from classmates. Additionally, the feedback provided by one classmate to another may not be accurate and may require review from the instructor.

PEER FEEDBACK IN ONLINE COURSEWORK

I value peer feedback as an evidence-based practice and have used it in various ways in most of my courses. I use it often in my online classes because it is an additional way for my students to build community. Many of our students are first generation college students and community is so important for their success.

—Jamie Colwell, PhD, Associate Professor

It is not surprising peer feedback is a common activity in online coursework (van Popta et al., 2017). It is an evidence-based practice that can be applied to any academic area. It can aid in the development of new ideas by presenting different approaches to the same course activities. Its design can leverage a range of digital tools (see Table 5.1 for a selection of tools for digital peer feedback) to make the sharing of candidate work easily accessible. And, as Jamie notes above, peer feedback can foster a sense of community in asynchronous learning environments, settings that can be isolating at times.

Since my courses are asynchronous, we do not have opportunities to engage in real-time conversations. Instead, like many online instructors, I try to replicate the back and forth of classroom dialogue by using the discussion board tool in my LMS. Of course, it is not exactly the same as synchronous discussions, but it does allow candidates to interact with course resources, consider the content, post perspectives, and engage in conversations with classmates. It also creates a space for all voices to be heard, especially those who may be hesitant to talk in a face-to-face class.

The content of these discussions includes conceptualizing information, analyzing it, and debating different perspectives. However, before candidates are ready to interact, they must first experience the content you intend to teach. Figure 5.1 details the steps to a series of activities I use to teach undergraduate elementary teacher education majors about Response to Intervention (RtI), an approach to differentiating instruction. The instructional chain concludes by inviting candidates to apply what they learned about RtI in feedback to classmates.

Most LMSs have embedded discussion boards that can be used to engage candidates in peer review. Another option is a dedicated peer review tool, which is available in some LMSs, such as Canvas. A peer review tool allows candidates to evaluate classmates' work either publicly or anonymously using a rubric uploaded by the instructor. Instructors could also choose to link to one of the many third-party tools, such as time-stamp video tools like Vialogues and TurboNote, that afford this kind of interactivity. No matter the tool, I have found preparing candidates to provide quality responses to classmates, the kind that constructively challenge the way one thinks about their work, to be the most difficult aspect of this type of practice.

Table 5.1. Digital Tools: Peer Feedback

Digital Tool	Purpose
Peergrade	Peer Feedback
Vialogues	Time-Stamp Video Tool
TurboNote	Time-Stamp Video Tool

Figure 5.1. Example Lesson of Peer Feedback in Response to Classroom Learning

Learning Objective:

* Compare and contrast approaches to implementing Response to Intervention (RtI) in math and reading at different grade levels.

Activities:

* Experience
    » Candidates watch a video lecture reviewing the components of Response to Intervention.
* Experience
    » Candidates watch three videos exemplifying approaches to implementing RtI in elementary, middle, and high school.
* Analyze
    » Candidates analyze the approaches presented in the videos for the purpose of identifying three elements of each approach: (1) differentiated instruction, (2) teacher collaboration, and (3) communication among all school personnel.
* Conceptualize
    » Candidates compare and contrast two of the three approaches presented in the videos and post their results in the discussion board.
* Apply
    » Candidates read classmates' posts comparing the same approaches and pose questions, extend thoughts, affirm ideas, or challenge statements.

Digital Tools:

* Video (all from RTI Action Network):
    » Implementing Response to intervention: Boulevard Elementary School: www.youtube.com/watch?time_continue=6&v=a2-DXXoenAg
    » Implementing Response to Intervention: Russell Middle School:
    » www.youtube.com/watch?time_continue=3&v=VlRM6kf7EZ0
    » Implementing Response to Intervention: Tigard High School: www.youtube.com/watch?v=YtTKuBZ-nvY
* LMS discussion board

Developing Peer Feedback Skills

* I completely agree with your points!
* Nice job with your blog. It is so colorful. How did you get the image on the right side? I had trouble reformatting.

- I never thought of the issue like the way you described. Thanks so much for the insights!

The feedback above was drawn directly from discussion board interactions between classmates in both undergraduate and graduate online courses. As you can see, they are all positive affirmations with little substance. I wish I could say they are rare. Instead, they reflect many conversations that took place in my courses before I started providing guidelines, and in some cases direct instruction, about what to include in peer feedback.

Feedback and Analysis

I began tackling the issue of substantive feedback in my course *Coaching Teachers*. It seemed like a good place to start since coaching requires teacher leaders to interact with other adults. Digital tools that enable interactivity, such as discussion boards, VoiceThread, and Flipgrid, were already staples in the course, so it was really a matter of designing a way to scaffold the substance of the peer feedback delivered by those tools. Unlike the immediacy of face-to-face classes, where instructors model, candidates practice, and instructors answer questions all within one class period, teaching in asynchronous environments takes place in steps where time lapses between interactions. Therefore, the challenge was to systematically prepare candidates to provide effective feedback beginning the first day of the online class.

After much thought, I created an assignment that incorporated a series of activities designed to build candidates' feedback skills through continuous practice and reflection. Feedback and Analysis was a two-part assignment that spanned the entire semester. It was introduced in the first course module to give candidates time to ask questions and plan for the activities within the course schedule. It also gave teachers a model that could be adapted for developing these important skills with K–12 students.

Part I, described in Figure 5.2, required candidates to complete a series of activities each week and post their work on the class website or on a third-party tool such as FlipGrid. At the end of the week, candidates were required to provide their classmates with feedback on their responses using coaching techniques taught in class (e.g., listening, paraphrasing, deliberate language).

The content of the feedback was described as:

- Substantive
- Referring directly to classmates' posts with debate, agreement, questions
- Sharing of diverse perspectives
- Supported by evidence

Deciding how to assess candidates' weekly feedback was challenging for a few reasons. I found that candidates did not always complete activities that did not have a grade attached, so I was compelled to allocate some weight to the weekly responses. Second, I wanted the overall process of composing feedback to be organic. In other words, at the end of the semester, I wanted candidates to see the evolution of their word choice, the types of comments they made, who they responded to, and the quantity of feedback, rather than placing strict requirements on what to say and how many times to say it. I decided the best approach would be to allocate one point for completing Part I of the peer feedback activity. This made it simple. If they gave feedback to one classmate or 10, they received one point. If they made no comments, they received a zero. Candidates commented

Figure 5.2. Part I: Feedback and Analysis Assignment

- Read and/or view different resources and reflect on a series of prompts on the class discussion boards or other tech tools such as FlipGrid or Padlet. You will typically earn 1 point for these reflections—sometimes more, depending upon the assignment.
- For most activities, draw upon the content learned in our weekly modules about coaching dialogue and building relationships (i.e., paraphrasing, listening, building trust) to respond to at least one classmate's response. You will earn 1 point for these responses.
  - » Your feedback to your classmates should be **substantive.**
  - » **Refer directly** to classmates' reflections with **debate**, **agreement**, **questions**, and/or **diverse perspectives**.
  - » Dig deeper into the content and include **evidence** to support your feedback.
  - » Your feedback may also include supportive comments like "I agree" or "Good point." However, these comments should not be the primary method of responding to their work.
  - » Supporting does not necessarily mean agreeing. You can support your classmates' thinking by sharing diverse perspectives.
  - » We encourage you to push yourself beyond your comfort zone when you provide feedback. Provide feedback to classmates who have **differing views.** How can you disagree constructively?

favorably on this decision. For instance, Jake, a high school physics teacher, reflected:

> Overall, these discussion posts were not terribly difficult to complete. I think this is due to the fact that we weren't necessarily graded on the content of our posts, but more on the fact that we completed them and were actively responding to the members of our groups in a timely manner. While for some people, this would serve as an excuse to do the bare minimum, I usually strive to be better than that, because I wouldn't get anything out of this course if I simply did the responses just for the sake of getting them done.

Part II of the assignment, illustrated in Figure 5.3, engaged candidates in a systematic reflection of their peer feedback.

Figure 5.3. Part II: Feedback and Analysis Assignment

- Review all of the responses you made to classmates. Carefully critique your language. We encourage you to be honest. You will not be graded on the quality of the feedback you provided to your classmates. Instead, you will be graded on how deeply you reflected on your feedback including your strengths and areas in need of improvement.
- A few things to keep in mind:
  - » Look for patterns in your feedback. For instance:
    - ✓ Did you tend to provide feedback to like-minded classmates?
    - ✓ Did you push yourself beyond your comfort zone and provide feedback to classmates who you thought needed clarification in their understanding of content?
    - ✓ Were you ever too critical? Were there instances you would like to go back and re-do?
    - ✓ Were you too nice when you should have been more direct?
    - ✓ Did you utilize content learned from course resources in your feedback? If yes, identify examples. If not, identify instances in which you could have done so.
  - » Write a 5–7-page, well-organized paper describing your analysis. Include:
    - ✓ At least two strengths
    - ✓ At least two areas in need of improvement
    - ✓ Direct links to course content discussed in class or other resources with in-text citations
    - ✓ An APA-formatted reference list at the end of the paper; include APA-formatted in-text citations
  - ✓ You may use pseudonyms when you include examples of specific feedback interchanges with classmates. However, since you will not be using real names, please be as specific as possible about the assignment so we understand the context to which you are referring in your paper.

Specifically, they were required to critique and identify patterns in the comments they made to classmates throughout the semester. I provided prompting questions to aid with the analysis. Next, candidates were asked to write a reflective essay describing their feedback's strengths and areas in need of improvement. Examples and direct connections to course content were required to support their statements.

Part II of the assignment met the crux of the learning objective, which was to strengthen candidates' communication skills, specifically their ability to provide constructive, substantive feedback. Therefore, the essay carried significant weight, as seen in the rubric in Table 5.2 on pp. 70–71.

You will notice that candidates were never graded on the substance of their feedback to classmates. This may seem counterintuitive, given the learning objective. However, the instruction was designed to foster reflective practice. Candidates were invited to a learning space that encouraged truthfulness, where they evaluated their own process of growth.

If looked at in isolation, much of the candidates' peer feedback seems overwhelmingly positive with little challenge toward other people's ideas. Yet viewing individual student feedback over the course of the semester tells a different story. In the excerpt below, Kathleen, an 8th-grade math teacher, explains the evolution of her word choice and an area she needed to improve upon:

Another major area of concern I found when analyzing my feedback was the lack of inquiry. In order to guide teachers' thinking, it will be important to understand their perspective and rationale more deeply, which requires thoughtful questions. As Garmston, Linder and Whitaker (1993) explain "When teachers talk out loud about their thinking, their decisions become clearer to them, and their awareness increases" (p.1). In my first 8 feedback posts, I don't ask one single question. In starting to outline this assignment a little early, I was able to think about what was missing from my feedback and start to take a lens of inquiry when responding to peers. For example, when responding to Donna and Erin in modules six and seven, I asked guiding questions and was able to delve deeper into their ideas and show interest and a desire to understand more clearly.

Tabitha, an instructional coach, explained how the assignment helped her identify strengths in her leadership style in the following essay excerpt:

Upon reflection, I was pleasantly surprised by the different types of feedback I provided. In general, I find that if something works, I tend to stick to it, even if it means repeating a certain style or approach. Given that, I was thinking that I would have probably gotten more comfortable with a certain style of feedback and defaulted to that more often than not. However, "tagging" the feedback that I gave during this course provided data for me to use. It turned out that while I only used the confrontational approach twice, the rest of the feedback "tags" were used fairly evenly.

Overall, I've been pleased with the outcomes of this activity and I encourage readers to consider implementing something similar. It transfers the evaluation of feedback to the candidates themselves through a scaffolded reflective practice that requires them to think deeply about their word choices, listening skills, and ability to respond to situations and ideas that reflect diverse perspectives. In turn, they can use what is learned from this experience in other online courses where they will undoubtedly be required to provide feedback to classmates. While the course under discussion here was for teacher coaches, feedback is a critical skill for teachers of K–12 students, and candidates pursuing other degrees, both at the graduate and undergraduate levels, will benefit from practice.

Scaffolding Peer Feedback

I recognize not all teacher education courses aim to build candidates' feedback skills as I do in the class *Coaching Teachers*. However, if instructors want to engage candidates in interactive and collaborative online activities and require responses to at least one classmate's post in a discussion board, then it is important to include scaffolds that lead to substantive feedback. In addition, many 3–12 teachers now require peer feedback of their students. Giving candidates structure, guidelines, and experience with peer feedback facilitates better teaching of it to their students. Below are tips for designing these types of activities.

- *Learning Objectives:* Like all activities, the first step is to identify the learning objective. In other words, why are candidates asked to provide peer feedback in the context of the lesson?
- *Define:* Since learners tend to provide surface-level comments rather than substantive feedback, it is always a good idea to define what you mean by peer feedback. Also, be sure to explain why you are requiring responses to classmates. Invest

Table 5.2. Feedback and Analysis Assignment Rubric

Criteria	Ratings		Total Points Possible
Introduction	Intro provides context for understanding the purpose of the paper.	Intro provides general statement about coaching but would benefit from detail to direct reader to the purpose of the paper.	There is no introduction or the purpose of the paper is never stated.	10 points
Strength #1	Strength is described in detail. At least one example from student's feedback is included to illustrate it. Direct link is made to course content. In-text citation is included. Context of the interaction is clear to the reader.	Strength is described but would benefit from more detail. Context of interaction may not be clear to the reader. At least one example from student's feedback is included. Link is made to course content but may benefit from more detail. In-text citation may not be included.	Strength is vaguely described or not included at all. No link to class content.	10 points
Strength #2	Strength is described in detail. At least one example from student's feedback is included to illustrate it. Direct link is made to course content. In-text citation is included. Context of the interaction is clear to the reader.	Strength is described but would benefit from more detail. Context of interaction may not be clear to the reader. At least one example from student's feedback is included. Link is made to course content but may benefit from more detail. In-text citation may not be included.	Strength is vaguely described or not included at all. No link to class content.	10 points

Area in Need of Improvement #1	Area in need of improvement is described in detail. At least one example from student's feedback is included to illustrate it. Direct link is made to course content. In-text citation is included. Context of the interaction is clear to the reader.	Area in need of improvement is described but would benefit from more detail. Context of interaction may not be clear to the reader. At least one example from student's feedback is included. Link is made to course content but may benefit from more detail. In-text citation may not be included.	Area in need of improvement is vaguely described or not included at all. No link to class content.	10 points
Area in Need of Improvement #2	Area in need of improvement is described in detail. At least one example from student's feedback is included to illustrate it. Direct link is made to course content. In-text citation is included. Context of the interaction is clear to the reader.	Area in need of improvement is described but would benefit from more detail. Context of interaction may not be clear to the reader. At least one example from student's feedback is included. Link is made to course content but may benefit from more detail. In-text citation may not be included.	Area in need of improvement is vaguely described or not included at all. No link to class content.	10 points
Professionalism	Paper is well-written, proofread with few, if any, spelling or grammatical errors. It is well-organized.	Paper would benefit from revision. Should be proofread for spelling and/or grammatical errors.	Paper is not considered professional due to large number of spelling and/or grammatical errors or paper is disorganized and difficult to follow.	6 points

your candidates in the practice so they understand how it can
build community, introduce diverse perspectives, and support
understanding of course content.

- **Model:** Although it is extremely time-consuming, I model
substantive feedback for my learners. I point out the types of
markers I want to see in their feedback, including:
  - » questions
  - » different viewpoints
  - » connections to course content
  - » challenges to their thinking
  - » additional resources
- **Rubric:** One rationale for using peer feedback is to provide a
midway check of learning performance before assignments are
submitted for evaluation. The best way to do this is to provide
a rubric like the general one shown in Table 5.3 that guides the
peer evaluation based upon the learning objectives. Candidates
can use the rubric as they draft feedback to their classmates. Be
sure the rubric language is consistent with your instruction on
the topic.

Table 5.3. Example of General Rubric for Providing Peer Feedback

Elements	Exceeds Expectations	Meets Expectations	Does Not Meet Expectations
Requirements	All assignment requirements were met with additional details.	All requirements were met.	Not all requirements were met.
Articulation of Points/Concepts	Candidate articulates content using descriptive, concise language and includes multiple examples to illustrate concepts.	Candidate articulates content, but more concise language should be used when describing certain concepts. Also, more detail or examples could be included.	Candidate's presentation of content should be revised to more clearly articulate content. Examples and details should be included.
Improvements	No improvements need to be made.	Only 1 or 2 improvements need to be made.	There are a lot of improvements that could be made.

- *Know the Limits:* Keep in mind that peers are not content experts. They are in the process of learning, just like their classmates; therefore, feedback may not be accurate. I recommend reminding candidates of this throughout the semester and encouraging them to contact you if questions arise about the accuracy of advice provided. More importantly, for this reason I do not ask candidates to grade their classmates in any of my courses, undergraduate or graduate. Instead, I allocate participation points for the timeliness and quality of the feedback.

YOUR TURN

This section is here to provide space to practice designing a series of activities that incorporate peer feedback. Use Table 5.4 to scaffold your design. A few reminders:

- Identify your learning objective(s). This will dictate the type of peer feedback you implement.
- Brainstorm activities candidates need to complete before and after they provide peer feedback.
- Identify the type(s) of knowledge processes associated with each activity.
- Determine if there are additional activities you could include to challenge candidates in different ways.
- Brainstorm digital tools that could be integrated into the activities. Will you require they use a particular tool or will you provide a menu of options? Also, consider the tools' affordances in light of the activities you are assigning.

SUMMARY

Many instructors use peer feedback to precipitate dialogue among candidates in online courses. Giving (and receiving) productive feedback is important for teachers' growth, but it is difficult to do. This chapter presented several ideas for preparing teacher candidates to share substantive comments with classmates. It includes assignment descriptions, student work samples, response prompts, and a scoring rubric to illustrate its many facets.

Table 5.4. Your Turn: Peer Review

Learning Objective(s)	Activities	Knowledge Processes	Digital Tools	Attributes of Digital Text

CHAPTER 6

Virtual Field Experience

Lynn, a junior studying social studies education, was asked to reflect on her recent field experience:

> My 6th-grade placement was wonderful, but I didn't see many of the teaching practices I learned about in my university methods class. Also, we didn't get much time to share what we observed in our placements when we met with our professor and other classmates. It felt like the two experiences weren't connected.

Teacher candidates I work with tell me fieldwork is the most exciting part of their program because they get to live and breathe the realities of the classroom. Many of them also express concerns similar to those described by Lynn. I understand the disconnect they mention, especially since I am responsible for teaching methods courses that incorporate field placements. For example, I teach an undergraduate course in educational technology, and all of the field-based assignments require some form of technology integration. Yet many of the classrooms where candidates are placed still do not have adequate technology access. Even where devices and reliable Internet connections are available, some clinical educators (CEs) merely use technology to replicate traditional teaching practices rather than model technology use in ways that transform instruction. Additionally, some teacher candidates report difficulty allocating time to try out their own tech-integrated lessons with students.

EVIDENCE-BASED PRACTICE: FIELD EXPERIENCE

Field experience provides teacher candidates with opportunities to apply content learned in university classes to their work with children and other educators in schools. A critical component of teacher preparation for both preservice and inservice educators, field experience comes in several forms (Cochran-Smith, Feiman-Nemser, McIntyre, & Demers,

2008). One type is observational, where teacher candidates serve only as outside observers. A second type places candidates in supporting roles where they help facilitate classroom teachers' instruction. A third type requires more engagement in the educational environment. In these field placements, candidates take responsibility for designing and implementing instruction in real-world settings. Student teaching, the most time-intensive, is lengthier, where candidates may co-teach (Soslau, Gallo-Fox, & Scantlebury, 2018) or take complete responsibility for all aspects of the classroom environment, such as weekly lesson planning, administration of assessments, and behavior management, for an entire semester or academic year (Ronfeldt, Reininger, & Kwok, 2013).

Although fieldwork has been a cornerstone of teacher preparation for many years, there are many factors that challenge its successful integration into university programs. For instance, field placements involve several stakeholders: candidates, clinical educators, and university supervisors and/or faculty. Many times, the expectations for those involved are not well-delineated, leading to confusion and miscommunication (Valencia, Martin, Place, & Grossman, 2009). In turn, candidates are caught between constituencies with different, and sometimes unexpressed, expectations. Another challenge is the potential for conflicting approaches to instruction. University instructors strive to prepare teacher candidates to understand, identify, and implement evidence-based practices (Scheeler, Budin, & Markelz, 2016). However, not all CEs model EBP or instruction as they are taught in the university classroom. A third challenge is simply the logistics surrounding placements and scheduling. Placements should reflect diverse settings, both geographically and by grade level. Transportation must be considered to ensure candidates can get to and from the schools. Even teaching schedules must be reviewed carefully, since some content, like social studies and science, may be taught only at certain times of the academic year.

VIRTUAL FIELD EXPERIENCE

To strengthen the field component of my courses, I implement a virtual field experience (VFE), an online placement where candidates interact with and observe skilled educators as they implement evidence-based instruction (see Table 6.1. for a selection of digital tools for VFE). Research (Karchmer-Klein, 2007) indicates several benefits to this virtual approach. First, it is not bound by the university's geographical location.

Table 6.1. Digital Tools for Virtual Field Experience

Digital Tool	Purpose
FlipGrid	Synchronous/asynchronous collaboration with universities/K–12 schools
Skype	Interviews/Mystery Skype
Zoom	Interviews

This allows instructors to connect candidates with educators who effectively model the concepts taught in their classes. Second, because classmates are engaged in the same situation with the same CE and/or K–12 students, they can collaboratively reflect on strengths and concerns and problem-solve issues. Third, the university instructor plays a vital role in the virtual field experience from the selection of CE to the instructional design. This, in turn, creates consistency between the university course and the placement. The virtual field experience leverages technology in ways that allow instructors to easily connect with teachers and resources all over the world while creating shared experiences for teacher candidates from which they can experience, conceptualize, analyze, and apply content.

Designing the Virtual Field Experience

The virtual field experience encompasses several steps conducted over the Internet. Interactions between participants can range from one class session to several weeks. They can also be designed in different forms. For instance:

- Examining one teacher's instruction through observations and interviews. No interaction with K–12 students.
- Instructing/collaborating with students in one K–12 classroom.
- Instructing/collaborating with multiple K–12 classrooms.
- Collaborating with or coaching candidates in teacher education courses at other universities.

In Figure 6.1, I describe general steps to designing a virtual field experience in a linear sequence. Keep in mind, however, the steps are typically implemented recursively since each, beyond identifying learning objectives, depends upon factors such as schedules, the number of students/candidates, and access to digital tools.

Figure 6.1. Steps to Virtual Field Experience

- Identify learning objectives
- Identify clinical educator(s)/partner classroom
- Design instruction
- Implement virtual field experience
- Collaborate

Identify Learning Objectives

The first step is to identify what you want your teacher education candidates to learn. The most accessible topics to consider are those already incorporated into the syllabus. For education methods courses, these tend to be content knowledge standards and strategies associated with teaching them. It is useful, however, to also think broadly when identifying learning objectives. Virtual field experiences connect people to places near and far, providing amazing opportunities to build global awareness and empathy toward others. For example, #LookUpChallenge is a project designed by students at Saline High School in Michigan. Its purpose is to increase inclusivity within communities. Using research to back their claims, students paint ceiling tiles that present statistics, quotes, and artwork that advocate for the reduction of inequalities such as gender, race, religion, and sexual orientation. The tiles are spread across their school to inform classmates of the issues under investigation. The project has a website (lookupchallenge.simplesite.com/443642004) and invites classrooms from around the world to join and share their research and student voices. This could be a great introductory virtual field experience for a teacher educator looking to connect candidates to high school students to explore important issues of diversity while also strengthening communication skills.

As with other activities described in this book, I also encourage instructors to consider how activities can support content area knowledge and technology competencies simultaneously. The virtual field experience lends itself well to both since digital tools are used to facilitate communication and to present content. Table 6.2 illustrates how content area learning objectives and ISTE technology standards for teachers can structure an online activity.

After identifying learning objectives, I consider the following questions, framed by the four knowledge processes (Cope & Kalantzis, 2015).

Table 6.2. Example of Meeting Math Content Standards and Technology Competencies

CCSS.Math. Content.2.OA.A.1	ISTE Standards for Educators 5: Designer	Digital Tool/ Activity Idea
Use addition and subtraction within 100 to solve one- and two-step word problems involving situations of adding to, taking from, putting together, taking apart, and comparing, with unknowns in all positions.	Design or adapt relevant learning experiences that incorporate digital tools and resources to promote student learning and creativity.	Candidate will use a screen capturing tool to model for students how to think aloud while solving one- and two-step word problems.

- How will my teacher education candidates experience content?
- How will my teacher education candidates conceptualize content?
- How will my teacher education candidates analyze content?
- How will my teacher education candidates apply content to a particular context?

I do not necessarily implement all of the activity types I construct in response to the questions above, and there is no preset order to completing the ones I do assign. Nevertheless, I find it useful to consider different approaches to teaching and then pare them down based upon time and the form of the virtual field experience I have chosen.

Identify Clinical Educators/Partner Classrooms

Like many faculty in schools of education, I am fortunate to work with an office of people who identify placements for our teacher education candidates. These colleagues are well versed in the characteristics of nearby school districts and know the excellent CEs who are effective mentors. Virtual field experiences differ from live placements in that university instructors are responsible for locating clinical educators and partner classrooms. Although it is time-consuming, I enjoy this step of the process. I am able to connect with CEs who live far away, but who demonstrate the types of practices that would benefit my students. Over the years I have collaborated with classrooms in Wisconsin, New York, New Jersey, Virginia, California, and Sydney, Australia.

There are several things to consider when identifying partners for a virtual field experience:

- Content knowledge: Is the CE well versed in the content you are teaching?
- Pedagogical knowledge: Will the CE effectively model evidence-based practices?
- Technology access: Does the CE have access to digital tools you want to utilize?
- Technology skills: Does the CE know how to use the digital tools you plan to use?
- Investment: Is the CE sufficiently interested in the project so deadlines are met?

There are several digital tools and websites that can facilitate connections with CE/partner classrooms for virtual field experiences. One of my favorites is #GridPals, powered by FlipGrid, a digital space where educators and students can meet up to discuss topics using video, audio, and images. #GridPals, created by K–12 instructional coach Bonnie McClelland, is the current version of pen pals. Once you have an educator login for FlipGrid, you can create a profile and connect your candidates to either university or K–12 classrooms located in any of 180 countries. Once you've made initial contact with another educator, you can begin the process of discussing your ideas for instructional design, including timelines, regularity of communication, and final products.

If you are new to the virtual field experience, I suggest inviting teachers with whom you have established relationships. This facilitates the process by encouraging regular contact and follow-through with activities. You'll learn what works and what you may need to do differently the next time, which will make the experience more powerful for your candidates.

Design Instruction

The virtual field experience thrives when design is a collaborative process between the teacher educator and the CE. I find it beneficial to collaborate after I've identified learning goals and conceptualized general ideas of the activities I would ideally like to include. Next, I talk with the CE(s) and discuss which activities could seamlessly be incorporated into their existing classroom curriculum. Much like the traditional practicum, if we ask teachers to implement instruction that does not match their typical practice, it will not happen.

Most of the virtual field experiences I've participated in have incorporated numerous activities, as they take place over the course of a few weeks or the entire semester. They also reflect collaborative and individual learning. Figure 6.2 is an example of an experience that connected candidates enrolled in an online course on reading assessment and instruction with skilled literacy specialists.

As demonstrated by this sequence of activities, candidates had multiple opportunities to engage with content using a variety of digital tools. Since this example was drawn from a fully online course, technology use was not an issue; they were already well acquainted with Canvas tools as well as Zoom. The literacy specialists were responsible for recording their instructional sessions and uploading video clips to the Canvas website. Likewise, these tasks were not challenging for them since technology skills were factored in when they were invited to participate in the practicum. CE who are not as tech-savvy may need more support.

Implement Field Experience

I wish I could say that if the previous steps to the virtual field experience were well planned, implementation would go smoothly. Unfortunately, it is not always the case. Rather, this seems to be the point where unanticipated events occur. While it is impossible to control the school day, there are a few recommendations to help counteract some potential challenges.

- *Provide explicit directions:* Participants in fully online courses rely on directions that are communicated through written language or short audio/video clips. They do not have opportunities to ask real-time clarifying questions. Over time I've learned that outlining directions step by step saves me time in the long run. I also ask a colleague or graduate assistant to follow the directions to test for accuracy and clarity before sharing them with others.
- *Provide models:* In the past I was hesitant to provide candidates with models of student work in both face-to-face and online courses. I found that many times students replicated the models rather than using them as tools to guide their own interpretations of assignments. However, in teaching online I have found that models can provide immediate clarification to those who are ready to get started. I include a statement in my directions reminding candidates that models should only be used as such and that their work should be original.

Figure 6.2. Virtual Field Experience with Two Literacy Specialists

Learning Objective:

- Candidates will compare and contrast systematic literacy instruction provided to children with documented reading difficulties.
- Candidates will design systematic literacy instruction for a child with documented reading difficulties.

ILA Standards for the Preparation of Literacy Professionals 2017:

- ILA 7.1: Candidates work with individual students to assess literacy strengths and needs, develop literacy intervention plans, create supportive literacy learning environments, and assess impact on student learning.
- ILA 7.2: Candidates collaborate with and coach peers and experienced colleagues to develop, reflect on, and study their own and others' teaching practices.

Activities:

- Experience
  - » Candidates interview two literacy specialists to understand their educational backgrounds, teaching experience, and theoretical views on teaching reading.
  - » Candidates observe two literacy specialists as they provide systematic instruction in word recognition to a child at their school.
- Conceptualize
  - » Candidates compare and contrast instructional practices observed in both settings for similarities and differences.
- Analyze
  - » Candidates analyze assessment data from a case study of a child with difficulties in word recognition.
- Apply
  - » Candidates apply what they know about evidence-based literacy practices in word recognition by designing a 3-day lesson plan for the case study child in response to assessment data.
  - » Candidates share lesson plans with a classmate to solicit peer feedback.

Digital Tools:

- Interviews and observations take place using Zoom, a video conferencing tool.
- Compare/contrast of teaching practices posted on Canvas Discussion Board tool.
- Written analysis submitted to course instructor through Canvas Assignments tool.
- Written lesson plans presented to classmate using Canvas Peer Review tool.
- Written or audio feedback provided to classmate using Canvas Peer Review tool.

- ***Provide specific deadlines:*** I recommend identifying specific due dates for each activity. This will help all participants plan their time.
- ***Be flexible:*** If you've taught in a K–12 school you know anything can happen during the school day, requiring a shift in plans and rescheduling of activities. Expect to change deadlines at some point during the semester. Also, when all communication takes place over the Internet, be prepared for loss of connectivity and other technical mishaps.

Collaborate

In my experience, one of the most powerful aspects of the virtual field experience is the collaborative problem-solving that takes place due to the shared learning environment. Working in the same placement with the same CE(s) and students permits candidates to relate to each other's experiences in ways they can't within traditional field placements where they are isolated in their own classrooms.

An example of this collaborative problem-solving took place in one of the first virtual field experience placements I designed. I was teaching a literacy development course for preservice teachers. We worked with a 1st-grade class, and each candidate was paired with a 1st-grade student. Over the course of the project, we all read the same text. After each chapter the candidates emailed questions to their young partners, hoping to precipitate thoughtful conversations about the story. One candidate, Dani, who did not have much experience with young children, was disappointed when her partner did not respond to most of the questions she posed. She brought the issue to her classmates on the class discussion board by sharing an example of one of the messages she sent. The message was written like a friendly letter and included five paragraphs that outlined her views of the chapter along with six questions for the child to consider. A classmate responded by asking Dani if she had considered the age and grade level of her partner. The classmate reminded Dani of earlier class conversations about audience awareness and its importance, especially when communicating over the Internet. This interchange began a grand conversation about literacy development and our expectations for student response. We talked about factors specific to communicating over the Internet, such as typing. Dani was reminded by her classmates that 1st-graders have limited typing skills and vocabulary, so it would be better for her to limit the length of her comments and number of questions and lower her expectations for his response.

YOUR TURN

This section provides space to draft ideas for a virtual field experience. As described in this module, there are a lot of moving parts. I suggest starting small by brainstorming a short-term project with a familiar clinical educator. As you gain experience, you can make the experience more complex by inviting a broader audience to participate. Use Table 6.3 to scaffold your design. A few reminders:

- Identify your learning objective(s). This will guide who you invite to participate in the experience.
- Brainstorm activities candidates need to complete before and after they interact with the case.
- Identify the type(s) of knowledge processes associated with each activity.
- Identify clinical educator(s).
- Determine if there are additional activities you could include to challenge candidates in different ways.
- Brainstorm digital tools that will be necessary to communicate with the participants. Make sure all participants are familiar with the ones you select.

SUMMARY

This chapter focuses on the importance of field experience within teacher education and proposes the idea of leveraging technology to offer additional opportunities to partner with other classrooms and educators. The virtual field experience is not a replacement for traditional face-to-face field experiences. There is nothing like the look, feel, smell, and inner workings of an actual classroom culture in action. Yet as coursework transitions to online delivery, it is useful to explore technology's potential for connecting teacher education candidates to authentic professional environments. Consider the virtual field experience a complement to the traditional approach, one that can add rich opportunities to practice the countless skills we want candidates to master.

With that said, I would be remiss if I did not admit the design and implementation of this type of field experience is demanding of time and patience. There are times when technology fails. I have had instances where I invited educators who did not meet deadlines or fulfill requirements of the project. In fact, there always seems to be a point in the process when

I pause and wonder why I continue to challenge myself with these experiences. When things do not go as planned, though, I remind myself of
the benefits of fieldwork and how important it is for candidates to have
opportunities to practice the strategies we teach in our courses.

Table 6.3. Your Turn: Virtual Field Experience

Learning Objective(s)	Activities	Knowledge Processes	Digital Tools	Attributes of Digital Text

PUTTING IT TOGETHER

CHAPTER 7

Big Picture

Teaching in an online environment has made me a better and more intentional instructor because it has forced me to think about what are the essential learning outcomes for a course, and to be more intentional about the kinds of activities, readings, and interactions I design to achieve those outcomes.

—Bill Lewis, PhD, Associate Professor

I think my favorite part of teaching is designing courses, and while in-person courses have flexibility in some ways, online courses allow you to really design the learning environment. I think about some of the (awful) rooms I've taught in. In an online course, I get to shape the environment in a much more direct way, from the look and feel of the course, to the ways I want students to interact with the material, to the kinds of tools I think foster better communication, engagement, and assessment. I find the environment almost richer than in person.

—Liz Farley-Ripple, PhD, Associate Professor

I am fortunate in that I coordinate and teach in fully online programs that were spearheaded by faculty. Instead of being directed by the administration, my colleagues and I were invited to design courses using the evidence-based practices we thought would be most rewarding to the candidates. When I began writing this book, I asked several of them to tell me what they most like about teaching online. Two of their responses open this chapter.

Designing online courses can be fun, time-intensive, and frustrating. To support readers who are new to this challenge or those who are interested in new ways of approaching online instruction, I explain the steps I take when designing courses and share a detailed example drawn from a graduate-level fully online course. I conclude the chapter by presenting five key principles that I think are important. They are drawn from my own experiences as well as from a host of online instructors I've had the honor of learning from over the years.

PUTTING THE PIECES TOGETHER

Designing online instruction is not a quick or easy task. Even after 17 years, I begin course design at least 4 months ahead of the start date if I am starting from scratch and creating videos that must be embedded into modules. I usually begin 2 months before the start date if I am redesigning a published course or tinkering with a few activities.

To me, the process is like putting together pieces of a puzzle. Each activity is part of a bigger module which is part of the overall course. I move around the pieces until they fit and the big picture comes into focus. The malleability of digital text lends itself to this recursive process, enabling me to change my mind or add more content, even midway through a semester.

The next few pages take readers step by step through my design process for the course Fostering Technology-Based Collaborations, a requirement of a fully online MEd in teacher leadership program. The process can be used when designing courses in any type of program, undergraduate or graduate.

Starting the Process

Just like any course, online course planning begins with reviewing the learning objectives. Sometimes they are dictated by professional organizations, and other times faculty have flexibility. Whichever the case, instructional design should begin with these objectives, so it is imperative they be identified at the start.

Our MEd in TL program is framed by the Teacher Leader Model Standards (2013) developed by the Teacher Leader Exploratory Consortium. Figure 7.1 lists the three standards met by the course used in this example.

Figure 7.1. Teacher Leader Model Standards for Fostering Technology-Based Collaborations Course

- Identify and use appropriate technologies to promote collaborative and differentiated professional learning.
- Use knowledge of existing and emerging technologies to guide colleagues in helping students skillfully and appropriately navigate the universe of knowledge available on the Internet, use social media to promote collaborative learning, and connect with people and resources around the globe.
- Use technology to represent and advocate for the profession in contexts outside of the classroom.

As you can see, these standards reflect a broad roadmap, not specific content. For instance, specific digital tools are not listed. Instead, as the instructor I can tap into my expertise in the area of digital literacies and educational technology to identify the tools I think would be most beneficial to focus on throughout the semester. I also identify the learning objectives that will guide my weekly instruction. To do this, I parse the standards into manageable chunks and consider the breadth and depth I want to delve into for each. I list the topics I believe are most relevant and corresponding learning objectives that can help drive the instructional design. I also figure out the best way to sequence the content within the 7-week time frame of the course. Table 7.1 lists the topics and learning objectives I identified through this initial process.

It is important to note that at this step of the planning process I have not yet identified technology tools to incorporate into the coursework. This is purposeful because I want a clear understanding of the topics and objectives before I decide how candidates will participate in class activities and represent their knowledge.

Designing Assignments and Activities to Meet Learning Objectives

The next step in my planning is to pinpoint activities and assignments I want to use to meet the learning objectives. I prefer to work backward by first identifying the assignments and then the activities that will lead up to their completion. For example, given the focus of this course, I decided to integrate an assignment that required candidates to create their own professional learning network (PLN). My rationale was that a PLN would teach candidates how to collaborate with educators outside of their school environment on a regular basis, teaching them that professional development could take place on their schedule. Designing a PLN over the 7-week course would give candidates time to identify important problems of practice, seek out important connections, and engage with educators beyond their school building who could provide potential solutions to the challenges they face. Table 7.2 is a completed assignment planning chart where I list all graded assignments from the course, an overview of their purpose, and percentage of the final grade.

After the assignments are identified, I decide on the sequence of topics so I can begin to work on the activities. I design one module at a time, keeping in mind the four knowledge processes (experiencing, conceptualizing, analyzing, applying) to make sure I provide candidates with a wide range of learning opportunities.

Table 7.1. Topics and Learning Objectives for Fostering Technology-Based Collaborations Course

Topics	Learning Objectives
Digital Identity	• Define the term *digital identity*. • Identify their digital identity by searching on the Internet and assess the positive and negative aspects presented. • Assess digital identities presented in a case study using evaluation methods discussed in class.
Cyber Safety	• Define the term *cyber safety*. • Report the policies and procedures for cyber safety in their professional setting.
Professional Learning Networks	• Identify and connect with professional organizations that provide solutions to Problems of Practice in their professional setting. • Identify niche groups that study on issues related to their PoP. • Using evaluation methods shared in class, evaluate digital content collected for their PLN. • Report their understanding of the purpose and benefits of professional learning networks.
Digital Tools	• Apply an evaluation tool to assess how digital tools can be used to collaborate with others.
Technology-Based Instructional Practices	• Compare and contrast four technology-based instructional practices and identify context for implementing them in professional development.
Models of Tech Integration	• Compare and contrast similarities and differences between two models of technology integration. • Assess an existing professional development session and modify it using knowledge of digital tools, models of tech integration, and instructional practices.
Reading and Writing in Digital Spaces	• Define multimodality, reading path, new literacies. • Describe principles of new literacies and critical media literacy. • Apply critical evaluation skills to websites.
Using Digital Tools to Promote Parent and Family Engagement	• Identify digital tools that can foster parent and family engagement with schools. • Recognize challenges associated with parent and family engagement with schools. • Use research to identify and report solutions to challenges associated with parent and family engagement with schools.

Table 7.2. Completed Assignment Planning Chart

Fostering Tech-Based Collaborations: Assignments			
Assignment	**Purpose**	**Due Date**	**% of grade**
PLN Assignment	Students will systematically build a PLN on a topic of their choice using technology.	Weekly	50%
PD Redesign	Students will revise a PD to follow a model of tech integration and include collaboration tools.	Module 4	15%
Screencast	Students will create a 1-minute screencast tutorial modeling how to use a digital tool to promote parent and family engagement in school activities.	Module 6	10%
Reflective Posts	Students will complete reflective posts on a range of topics.	Weekly	25%

For example, I chose to cover digital identity in Module 1 of the course. I made a list of subtopics associated with it and then researched them by reviewing literature published in research and practitioner journals. Since the course would be delivered online, I also searched for videos and podcasts on sites such as TED.com, NPR.org, and blogs I visit frequently so that I could provide candidates with a range of resources to help them experience the concept. After curating several readings and videos, I brainstormed ways to engage candidates in activities that would require them to analyze, conceptualize, and apply what they learned. I found a teacher-created activity posted on Common Sense Media titled *Trillion Dollar Footprint*. The lesson was a case study that required candidates to participate in a scenario in which they served as a TV producer and were in the process of hiring one of two people who applied for the same job. They were given information about each applicant's digital identity found on social media sites. The candidates were to use the information to make a hiring decision and then provide a rationale for their choice. The sequence of activities for teaching the topic of digital identity is illustrated in Figure 7.2.

Figure 7.2. Digital Identity Activities

Learning Objectives:

- Define the term *digital identity*.
- Identify their digital identity by searching on the Internet and assess the positive and negative aspects presented.
- Assess digital identities presented in a case study using evaluation methods discussed in class.

Activity: Experience

- Watch: Brown, P. (2015). *Towards A Digital College Student Development Theory*. In this video, Brown discusses his research on digital identity with college students. Although the presentation focuses on young adults, the points are applicable to anyone developing identity with and through digital tools.

Activity: Experience

- Take a moment and search the digital identity/identities you present on the Internet.
- Start by searching for yourself using different search engines: Google, Bing, and Pipl.
- If you are a high school or college instructor, search for yourself on www.ratemyteachers.com/ or www.ratemyprofessors.com/
- Look at your social media accounts and consider the identity/identities you portray to others. What types of things do you post? How do you categorize them: family, work, hobbies, etc.?
- Take note of what you've found and categorize your findings as:
  - » Acceptable (leave it alone)
  - » Neutral (ignore it/not worth worrying about)
  - » Unacceptable (Oh no! Time to delete!)

Activity: Conceptualize, Analyze, Apply

- Take on the role of TV producer and identify a new host for a reality talent show. You've hired a private investigator to conduct Internet searches on two candidates to uncover their digital identities. You will use this material to make your hiring decision. Additionally, you will use VoiceThread to respond to a series of reflection prompts. As you do, think about how VoiceThread can be used to foster collaboration among educators.
- Read the candidates' bios and online documents, complete the feedback form, and decide which candidate to hire and why.
- For this part of the assignment you will report your hiring choice in a small group of classmates on VoiceThread and then discuss your decisions and rationales.

This culminating activity engaged candidates in a range of knowledge processes, supporting the first two activities completed at the beginning of the module.

Appendix A is a completed copy of a course organization chart that documents all 7 weeks of the course Fostering Technology-Based Collaborations. I use this document to organize my thoughts and maintain it as a digital copy so I can build on it throughout the course design process, resulting in an ever-changing document that illustrates alignment between learning objectives, activities, materials, and graded assignments. A blank downloadable copy of the chart can be found on the companion website: improvingonlineteachered.com.

Finalizing a Course

I publish my courses the Friday before classes begin. I find this very helpful for three reasons. First, it ensures candidates can log on prior to the semester commencing. This is especially important because online courses move quickly. Second, it gives me time to clarify information, answer questions, or fix issues they notice. Third, it provides candidates with time to get a feel for the course design and expectations before they become overwhelmed with the stresses of the semester. Truthfully, my online courses are never completely finalized. I stay very involved in my candidates' participation and if I find there are concepts they do not understand, I will add additional resources, activities, or virtual meetings with me.

KEY PRINCIPLES

In preparation for this book, I reviewed pages and pages of notes I took over the years as I planned my online instruction. I revisited course evaluations to remind myself of student views of my course design, its strengths, and areas in need of improvement. I also chose to invite others into the process of reflection to explore different perspectives of online learning. The result of this compilation of information is a list of key principles to consider when designing online courses. Many of them stem from blunders that colleagues or I have experienced, and some carry more weight than others when making instructional decisions.

5 Key Principles for Online Course Design

1. Design instruction for online environments
2. Assign grade value to important course activities
3. Differentiate instruction
4. Respect diversity in the online classroom
5. Continue professional development

Design Instruction for Online Environments

> My major mistake was thinking I could take any activity that was successful in a brick and mortar class and just transfer it online.
>
> —Elizabeth Soslau, PhD, Associate Professor

When applying to one of the two fully online programs I coordinate, applicants are required to write an essay on why they want to complete their degree online and why they want to pursue it at our university. The most common answers are convenience and our school's reputation for providing rigorous graduate programs in education. As program coordinator, it has been my mission to meld these expectations. Truthfully, it has not always been easy. Many faculty new to online teaching think instruction can transfer from face-to-face classrooms to digital environments. However, this isn't the case. Convenience in online learning means permitting candidates to work at their own pace, allowing them to take on the role of self-directed learner where they decide how deeply they participate, advocate for support when needed, and interject their voice when they have something to share. The instructor's responsibility then is to design instruction that meets candidates' expectations while also meeting the rigors of the field.

This is the reason I wrote this book. After years of practice, I have identified ways of integrating EBP that have been proven effective in traditional teaching spaces, with technology in ways that fosters interaction and collaboration among and between classmates and instructors. By carefully designing instruction that combines EBP, such as think alouds, case-based instruction, peer review, and virtual experiences, with digital tools instructors can create effective learning environments where candidates can work at their own pace, while also benefitting from effective online instructional practices. In the absence of such design, candidates are subjected to courses that rely on didactic activities.

Assign Grade Value to Important Course Activities

> If you think the assignment is absolutely necessary for students to develop the competencies you've set for the course, assign points to it! Even the most diligent and devoted students will overlook or dismiss suggested readings or group discussions if they are not evaluated on it.
>
> —Jamie Colwell, PhD, Associate Professor

The topic of grading was common among the instructors I talked to about their online design. They said that they used the promise (or threat) of grades to motivate participation, but did not want to overload candidates, or themselves, with graded activities. While we do not allocate points to everything candidates say and do in our face-to-face classes, the online classroom is different. Motivation can be difficult to foster in online environments, and I've heard from candidates that it is easy to skip assignments because they do not feel the same level of accountability as they would were they to see their instructors weekly.

Yet it is extremely time consuming to grade every submission. I recommend finding a balance. As Jamie suggests, if an activity is critical to student learning, then assessments should be required. Conversely, activities that are less than vital may be left without assessment. Draw on the EBPs shared in this book for ideas on engaging your students thoughtfully and creatively with the goal of drawing them in to the content whether or not grades are attached.

Jaime True Daley, EdD, an assistant professor, pointed out another issue related to grading. She stated, "Don't assume students read the syllabus, directions, rubrics or model assignments." This happens in face-to-face classes all the time, but it can really affect candidates' performance in an online course because the instructor may not realize it until 2 or 3 weeks into the semester. To counteract this concern, we assign a Module 0 in all online courses. This series of activities includes:

- Overview of the course
- Directions on using the LMS
- Quiz on the syllabus
- Public space to post questions throughout the semester for the instructor
- Student lounge where students introduce themselves the first week
- Overview of larger projects

- Directions on how to access library resources
- Directions on how to format using APA
- Introduction to all technology tools used in course activities besides the LMS

Module 0 is required, and some of my colleagues choose to lock all other assignments in the LMS until Module 0 is completed. This assures them that candidates have at least skimmed the site and completed activities that were allotted points.

Differentiate Instruction

> One of the challenges I've confronted was deciding how to meet students where they are—to differentiate. I want to be able to plan for a variety of background knowledge.
>
> —Liz Farley-Ripple, PhD, Associate Professor

Differentiating instruction is difficult to plan for in an asynchronous class where you never meet candidates face to face, or you talk to them briefly using a video conferencing tool. To further compound the issue, it is a challenge to respond to candidates in real time to clear up misconceptions about content. If candidates are truly struggling, I will either make an appointment to talk with them or ask them to create a digital think aloud to verbalize their process of applying content learned in class. Together these methods give me insight into their thinking and ideas for scaffolding their learning.

Liz suggested an alternative solution. She explained:

> I ended up redesigning each module to include a quiz and a variety of activities that were differentiated by skill levels. The quiz (points for completion, but not correct/incorrect answers) would inform students of which of the 4 differentiated activities in the following activity would be most appropriate for them, given their scores. This gave everyone an opportunity to build new knowledge and learning opportunities tailored toward everyone, not just the "average" student.

Respect Diversity in the Online Classroom

Online learning environments are powerful conduits to meeting the needs of and building respect for diverse populations of learners. Many LMSs, such as Canvas, support a range of digital tools to ensure productive experiences for everyone. These include screen readers, keyboard shortcuts, closed captioning, and the ability to individualize quizzes. Online learning can also be designed in such a way that diverse perspectives are regularly brought into the classroom. Since geography does not prohibit candidates from pursuing online degrees, programs can consist of dynamic communities of learners who represent wide ranges of places and views about the world.

Even if your student enrollment does not reflect much diversity, technology can be used to invite global voices into classroom conversations. For instance, one of the first tasks I do when beginning my online course design is to identify experts in the field of study and invite them to be interviewed for the course. I ask them to audio- or video-record their responses to a range of questions we will tackle over the semester. I post these in the modules that relate to the topic. This extra effort of bringing in outside voices exposes candidates to perspectives they otherwise would not have opportunities to learn from.

In sum, online courses can be designed to meet the needs of diverse sets of learners or teach candidates how to do so in their own teaching. The challenge, however, is for faculty to design courses that do just that.

Elizabeth Soslau teaches online courses on issues related to equity and diversity. I asked her how she approaches these topics in her online courses, and she was emphatic that the most effective way is to build a safe community from the first day of class. She explained:

> I begin to build community from the beginning of class. Teaching about issues such as racial bias and other types of discrimination can bring up a lot of negative feelings in students. In the online environment, building community and safety was a challenge for me. I had to proactively anticipate, and problem solve for, students' feelings of shame and guilt when confronted with their own implicit biases. For example, for the implicit bias activity, students take an online implicit bias test published by Harvard University. Often the results are difficult to accept, especially for my white students. To normalize potentially stressful and embarrassing feelings, I embedded a series of YouTube clips that depict other people taking the implicit bias test. In the clips, participants openly share their feelings before, during, and after the test. I also include a description of my own disappointed feelings when I took the test. The reflective prompts then ask my students to compare and contrast their emotions, reactions, and sense-making processes with those

depicted in the video clips. This process helps students feel less alone and open up about their genuine reactions. Some students even described feeling grateful that they were not singled out for their results and that they felt "better" knowing that others had similar experiences.

Continue Professional Development

Many university faculty, myself included, allocate a portion of their time to providing professional development. We participate in conference presentations, work directly with educators in school-related settings, and serve professional organizations. With all of these activities, we sometimes overlook the need to strengthen our own skills, especially when we tackle a new challenge, like online course design.

A recent survey (Straumsheim, Jaschik, & Lederman, 2015) of university faculty indicated most are unaware of how to utilize their learning management system's digital tools to teach content using evidence-based teaching practices (Graham, Harris, & Chambers, 2016). These results are not surprising, given that few higher education faculty receive training in online teaching methods or instructional design (Ko & Rossen, 2017). Instead, pedagogical decisionmaking tends to be influenced by on-the-job experience or how faculty recollect their own learning experiences as students (Oleson & Hora, 2014).

How can faculty learn to teach online while also fulfilling the many other professional obligations that are part of the job description? One approach is to read blogs and subscribe to newsletters. Some of my favorites related to education are: *The Principal of Change* (georgecouros.ca/blog/), *Cult of Pedagogy* (www.cultofpedagogy.com/), and *Faculty Focus* (www.facultyfocus.com/). I also recommend leveraging social media tools such as Twitter and Voxer to build a *professional learning network* (PLN), a digital interactive space to connect with university faculty, K–12 teachers, content experts, professional organizations, and other stakeholders who can enrich your professional practice. For instance, I follow over 100 education-related professionals on Twitter and when I pose a question on my Tweeter feed, within 30 minutes I will have at least 20 responses.

If you teach online, I strongly encourage you to begin your own PLN. You can start by connecting to professional organizations that relate to your areas of interest. From there, I suggest you connect with other educators who post about topics of interest. To me it seems for every person I directly connect with over Twitter, I am introduced to five more individuals with similar interests. Keep in mind there is an unspoken rule about

PLN. Not only should you learn from others, but you should be sharing your knowledge too.

SUMMARY

As more education programs transition to online delivery, whether hybrid or full, it is imperative that faculty keep up with the pedagogical and technological skills necessary to design high-quality instruction. This can only be done if they are willing to learn more about digital environments, including digital text, affordances and constraints of digital tools, and new ways of integrating evidence-based practices. The ideas and lessons shared in this book are one facet of the knowledge needed. My hope is this book encourages readers to move forward with online instruction that is evidence-based, interactive, and collaborative.

Completed Course Organization Chart

On the following pages is a completed course organization chart that documents all 7 weeks of the course Fostering Technology-Based Collaborations. I use this document to organize my thoughts and maintain it as a digital copy so I can build on it throughout the course design process, resulting in an ever-changing document that illustrates alignment between learning objectives, activities, materials, and graded assignments. A blank downloadable copy of the chart can be found on the companion website: improvingonlineteachered.com.

Week	Objectives	Content/Activities
M1: Digital Identity, Cyber Safety, and Intro to PLNs	**By the end of this module, you will be able to:** • Define the terms *digital identity* and *cyber safety.* • Evaluate your digital identity. • Explain the policies and procedures for cyber safety in your professional setting. • Demonstrate how digital identities may affect professional opportunities. • Identify a Problem of Practice in your professional setting that you will explore through a PLN.	**Digital Identity:** • *Watch:* Brown, P. (2015). Towards a digital college student development theory. Retrieved from https://www.youtube.com/watch?v=GRhQWZLu2No&feature=youtu.be • *Search:* Digital Identity • *Complete:* Trillion Dollar Footprint Cyber Safety: • *Watch:* Mozilla. (2010). *How to choose strong passwords.* Retrieved from https://www.youtube.com/watch?v=COU5T-Wafa4&feature=emb_logo • *Read:* Cyber Safety Policies • *Research:* District Policies Where in the World? • *Listen:* Solomon, N. (2011). Friendly advice for teachers: Beware of Facebook. Retrieved from https://www.npr.org/2011/12/07/143264921/friendly-advice-for-teachers-beware-of-facebook • *Read:* Nast. J. (n.d.). Teacher's place in a cyber world: The "can's and can not's" as a state employee. Retrieved from https://www.smore.com/ke2e9-a-teacher-s-place-in-a-cyber-world • *Read:* Mettler, K. (2016). 'Poor Gorilla': Teacher's aide fired for racist Facebook posts about Michelle Obama. *The Washington Post.* Retrieved from www.washingtonpost.com/news/morning-mix/wp/2016/10/04/poor-gorilla-teachers-aide-fired-for-racist-facebook-posts-about-michelle-obama/ • *Watch:* OK City Teacher: https://kfor.com/2016/02/29/oklahoma-city-teachers-powerful-open-letter-about-the-struggles-of-teaching-is-gaining-attention-online/ • *Respond:* Where in the World activity. *PLN Part I: PoP*

M2: Digital Tools	**By the end of this module, you will be able to:** • Examine a range of digital tools and evaluate how they can be used to collaborate with others. • Identify and connect with professional organizations that provide solutions to Problems of Practice in your professional setting.	Twitter: • *Read:* Nations, D. (2019). What is microblogging? A definition of microblogging with examples. Retrieved from https://www.lifewire.com/what-is-microblogging-3486200 • *Create:* Twitter account Social Bookmarking : • *Watch:* Social bookmarking in plain English. Retrieved from www.youtube.com/watch?v=HeBmvDpVbWc&feature=youtu.be • *Research:* Diigo, Pinterest, Evernote, Feedly ***Backchanneling:*** • *Read:* Holland, B. (2014). The Backchannel: Giving every student a voice in the blended mobile classroom. Retrieved from https://www.edutopia.org/blog/backchannel-student-voice-blended-classroom-beth-holland ***Podcasting:*** • *Read:* Smythe, S., & Neufeld, P. (2010). "Podcast time": Negotiating digital literacies and communities of learning in a middle years ELL classroom. *Journal of Adolescent and Adult Literacy, 53*(6), 488–497. • *Read:* Brady-Myerov, M. (2019). Why podcasting is #trending since 'Serial' and why your class should be doing it. Retrieved from https://www.edsurge.com/news/2019-11-05-why-podcasting-is-trending-since-serial-and-why-your-class-should-be-doing-it Using Backchanneling and Podcasting in PD • *Listen and Tweet:* soundcloud.com/mcilab/s2-episode-02-tap-out-bedu0202 ***PLN Part II: Identify Professionals***

Week	Objectives	Content/Activities
M3: Tech-Based Instructional Practices	**By the end of this module, you will be able to:** • Describe how technology can be used to support research-based instructional practices. • Present a variety of digital tools that foster collaboration. • Identify niche groups that study on issues related to your PoP.	**Tech-Integrated Practices:** • *Read:* Coiro, J., Castek, J., & Quinn, D. J. (2016). Personal inquiry and online research. *The Reading Teacher, 69*(5), 483–492. • *Read:* Vasinda, S. (2020). Discussion before the discussion in virtual study groups: Social reading and open annotation. In R. Karchmer-Klein & K. Pytash (Eds.), *Effective practices in online teacher preparation for literacy educators,* Hershey, PA: IGI Global. **Explore Digital Tools:** • *View and Practice:* Hart, J. (2019). Top 200 tools for learning 2019. Retrieved from https://www.toptools4learning.com/ **PLN Part III: Identify Niche Groups**
M4: Models of Tech Integration	**By the end of this module, you will be able to:** • Describe models of technology integration. • Compare and contrast models of technology integration. • Assess existing PD and modify using knowledge of digital tools, models of tech integration, and instructional practices. • Identify professionals who study and can provide solutions to your PoP.	**Models of Tech Integration:** • *Watch:* Common Sense Media. (2016). Introduction to the TPACK Model. Retrieved from https://www.commonsense.org/education/videos/introduction-to-the-tpack-model • *Read:* Harris, J. & Hofer, M. (2009). Grounded tech integration. *Learning and Leading with Technology. 37*(2), 22–25. • *Read:* Hutchison, A., & Woodward, L. (2013). A planning cycle for integrating digital technology into literacy instruction. *The Reading Teacher, 67*(6), 455–464. • *Read:* Watulak, S. L., & Kinzer, C. K. (2013). Beyond technology skills: Toward a framework for critical digital literacies in pre-service technology education. In J. Avila & J. Pandya (Eds.), *Critical digital literacies as social praxis: Intersections and challenges* (pp. 127–153). New York, NY: Peter Lang. **PLN Part IV:** Identify PLN Buddies and Mentors

| M5: Reading and Writing in Digital Spaces | **By the end of this module, you will be able to:**
• Define multimodality, reading path, new literacies.
• Describe principles of new literacies and critical media literacy.
• Apply critical evaluation skills to websites.
• Evaluate digital content collected for your PLN. | **Reading and Writing:**
• *Read*: Leu, D. J., Jr., Kinzer, C. K., Coiro, J., Castek, J. & Henry, L. A. (2017). New literacies: A dual-level theory of the changing nature of literacy, instruction, and assessment. *Journal of Education, 197*(2), 1–18.
• *Read*: Serafini, F. (2015). Multimodal literacy: From theories to practices. *Language Arts, 92*(6), 412–423

Critical Literacies
• *Read*: Kellner, D., & Share, J. (2005). Toward critical media literacy: Core concepts, debates, organizations, and policy. *Discourse: Studies in the Cultural Politics of Education, 26*(3), 369–386.
• *Read*: Yglesias, M. (2016). Facebook's fake news problem is way bigger than fake news. Vox. Retrieved from www.vox.com/policy-and-politics/2016/11/18/13665938/fake-news-pepsi
• *Watch*: Pariser, E. (2011). *Beware online filter bubbles.* Retrieved from www.youtube.com/watch?v=B8ofWFx525s&feature=youtu.be
• *Watch*: Johnson U Wales University Library. (2011). *Evaluating information using the CRAAP test.* Retrieved from www.youtube.com/watch?v=1AWhE0mj69I
• *Reflect*: Analyze at least one website using the CRAAP method.

PLN Part V: Be Critical |

Week	Objectives	Content/Activities
M6: Using Digital Tools to Promote Parent and Family Engagement	**By the end of this module, you will:** • Identify digital tools that can foster parent and family engagement with schools. • Recognize challenges associated with parent and family engagement with schools. • Identify solutions to challenges associated with parent and family engagement with schools. • Use screencasting to provide parents/guardians with insight into using digital tools for home–school collaboration. • Report lessons you learned about PLNs. • Provide feedback to classmates on their PLN development and implementation.	***Parent Engagement:*** • *Read:* Quick Brief on Family Engagement in ESSA of 2015: Retrieved from ra.nea.org/wp-content/uploads/2016/06/FCE-in-ESSA-in-Brief.pdf • *Read:* Juniu, S. (2009). Computer mediated parent-teacher communication. *Actualidades Investigativas en Educación, 9*(3), 11–10. • *Read:* Wessling, S. B. (2012). Emailing parents: How to avoid unintended consequences. Retrieved from www.teachingchannel.org/blog/2012/09/20/emailing-parents/ • Research: Digital tools for support with parents • Create: Design a screencast using a tool of your choice to inform parents about how to use a digital tool to communicate with you at school. ***Challenges:*** • Choose a challenge • Research Solutions • Report by Sunday ***PLN Part VI:*** Share
M7: Professional Learning Networks	**By the end of this module, you will:** • Create a presentation or write a paper that illustrates your understanding of professional learning networks.	• ***PLN Part VII:*** Bringing It All Together

Description of Digital Tools Referenced in This Text

Title	URL	Description
30hands	30hands.com/	Multimodal presentation tool
AnswerGarden	answergarden.ch/	Backchannel tool
Audacity	www.audacityteam.org/	Open source audio editor
AudioNote	luminantsoftware.com/apps/audionote-notepad-and-voice-recorder/	Notepad and audio recorder
Backchannel Chat	backchannelchat.com/	Backchannel tool
Camtasia	www.techsmith.com/video-editor.html	Screen capture and video editing tool
Chatzy	www.chatzy.com/	Private backchannel tool
Explain Everything	explaineverything.com/	Multimodal whiteboard tool
FlipGrid	info.flipgrid.com/	Video collaboration tool
GarageBand	www.apple.com/mac/garageband/ www.garagebandforpc.com/	Music creation tool
Glogpedia	edu.glogster.com/glogpedia/	Multimodal presentation tool
GoReact	get.goreact.com/	Video feedback tool
Padlet	padlet.com/	Collaborative multimodal bulletin board tool
Peergrade	www.peergrade.io/	Peer review tool
Poll Everywhere	www.polleverywhere.com	Real-time polling tool
Question Cookie	www.questioncookie.com/	Backchanneling tool

Title	URL	Description
Quicktime	support.apple.com/quicktime	Screen capture tool/Video creation
Screencastify	www.screencastify.com/	Screen capture tool
Screen-cast-o-matic	screencast-o-matic.com/	Screen capture tool
Show Me	www.showme.com/	Multimodal whiteboard tool
Skype	www.skype.com/en/	Virtual field experience
Soundtrap	www.soundtrap.com/	Music creation tool
Toontastic	https://toontastic.withgoogle.com/	Multimodal presentation tool
TurboNote	turbonote.com/	Video feedback tool
Twiddla	www.twiddla.com/	Multimodal whiteboard tool
Twitter	twitter.com/	Backchanneling tool
Vialogues	www.vialogues.com/	Video feedback tool
Vittle Lite	www.qrayon.com/home/vittle/	Multimodal whiteboard
VoiceThread	https://voicethread.com/	Multimodal presentation tool
Zoom	https://zoom.us/	Virtual field experience

References

Allen, I. E., & Seaman, J. (2016). *Online report card: Tracking online education in the United States.* Babson Survey Research Group: Babson Park, MA. Retrieved from files.eric.ed.gov/fulltext/ED572777.pdf

American Library Association. (2013). Digital literacy, libraries, and public policy: Report of the Office for Information Technology Policy's Digital Literacy Task Force. Retrieved from districtdispatch.org/wp-content/uploads/2013/01/2012_OITP_digilitreport_1_22_13.pdf

Baker, E. A., Pearson, P. D., & Rozendal, M. S. (2010). Theoretical perspectives and literacy studies: An exploration of roles and insights. In E. A. Baker (Ed.), *The new literacies* (pp. 1– 22). New York, NY: Guilford Press.

Banse, H., Palacios, N. A., Merritt, E. G., & Rimm-Kaufman, S. E. (2017) Scaffolding English language learners' mathematical talk in the context of Calendar Math. *The Journal of Educational Research, 110*(2), 199–208, doi:10.1080/0022 0671.2015.1075187

Beach, R., & O'Brien, D. (2015). Fostering students' science inquiry through app affordances of multimodality, collaboration, interactivity, and connectivity. *Reading & Writing Quarterly, 31*(2), 119–134.

Bereiter, C., & Bird, M. (1985). Use of thinking aloud in identification and teaching of reading comprehension strategies. *Cognition and Instruction, 2*(2), 131–156.

Boscolo, P., & Ascorti, K. (2004). Effects of collaborative revision on children's ability to write understandable narrative texts. In L. Allal, L. Chanquoy, & P. Largy (Eds.), *Revision: Cognitive and instructional processes* (Vol. 13, pp. 157– 170). Boston, MA: Kluwer.

Butrymowicz, S. (2012). Can the burgeoning world of online teacher training improve public education? *The Hechinger Report.* Retrieved from hechingerreport.org/can-the-burgeoning-world-of-online-teacher-training-improve-public-education/

Castek, J., & Beach, R. (2013). Using apps to support disciplinary literacy and science learning. *Journal of Adolescent and Adult Literacy, 56*(7), 554–564.

Castek, J., Beach, R., Cotanch, H., & Scott, J. (2014). Examining middle-school students' uses of Diigo annotations to engage in collaborative argumentative writing. In R. Anderson & C. Mims (Eds.), *Handbook of research on digital tools for writing instruction in K–12 settings* (pp. 80–101). Hershey, PA: IGI Global.

111

Cazden, C. (2006, January). *Connected learning: "Weaving" in classroom lessons.* Keynote address presented at the Pedagogy in Practice 2006 Conference, University of Newcastle, Newcastle, UK.

Cho, K., & MacArthur, C. (2011). Learning by reviewing. *Journal of Educational Psychology, 103*, 73–84.

Choi, I., & Lee, K., (2009). Designing and implementing a case-based learning environment for enhancing ill-structured problem-solving: Classroom management problems for prospective teachers. *Educational Technology Research and Development, 57*(1), 99–129.

Cochran-Smith, M., Feiman-Nemser, S., McIntyre, D. J., & Demers, K. (2008). *Handbook of research on teacher education: Enduring questions in changing contexts.* New York, NY: Routledge.

Coiro, J. (2011). Talking about reading as thinking: Modeling the hidden complexities of online reading comprehension. *Theory to Practice, 50*(2), 107–115.

Coiro, J., & Dobler, E. (2007). Exploring the online reading comprehension strategies used by sixth-grade skilled readers to search for and locate information on the Internet. *Reading Research Quarterly, 42*(2), 214–257.

Cope, B., & Kalantzis, M. (2015). The things you do to know: An introduction to the pedagogy of multiliteracies. In B. Cope & M. Kalantzis (Eds.), *A pedagogy of multiliteracies: Learning by design* (pp. 1–36). New York, NY: Palgrave MacMillan.

Dietz, C.M., & Davis, E.A. (2009). Preservice elementary teachers reflection on narrative images of inquiry. *Journal of Science Teacher Education, 20*, 219–243.

Dorl, J. (2007). Think aloud! Increase your teaching power. *Young Children, 62*(4), 101–105.

Dymock, S. (2007). Comprehension strategy instruction: Teaching narrative text structure awareness. *The Reading Teacher, 61*(2), 1–167. doi:10.1598/RT.61.2.6

Ebner, R., & Ehri, L. (2013). Vocabulary learning on the Internet: Using a structured think-aloud procedure. *Journal of Adolescent & Adult Literacy, 56*(6), 472–481.

Ertmer, P. A., & Koehler, A. A. (2018). Facilitation strategies and problem space coverage: Comparing face-to-face and online case-based discussions. *Educational Technology Research and Development, 66*, 639–670.

Ertmer, P. A., & Russell, J. D. (1995). Using case studies to enhance instructional design education. *Educational Technology, 35*(4), 23–31.

Fitton, L., McIlraith, A. L., & Wood, C. L. (2018). Shared book reading: Interventions with English learners: A meta-analysis. *Review of Educational Research, 88*(5), 712–751.

Garmston, R., Linder, C., & Whitaker, J. (1993). Reflections on cognitive coaching. *Educational leadership, 51*(2).

Graham, S., Harris, K., & Chambers, A. B. (2016). Evidenced-based practice and writing instruction. In C. A. MacArthur, S. Graham, & J. Fitzgerald. (Eds.), *Handbook of Writing research* (Vol. 2) (pp. 211–226.). New York, NY: Guilford Press.

Hammerness, K., Darling-Hammond, L., & Shulman, L. (2002). Toward expert thinking: How curriculum-case writing prompts the development of theory-based professional knowledge in student teachers. *Teaching Education, 13*(2), 219–243.

Harris, J., & Hofer, M. (2009). Grounded tech integration. *Learning and Leading with Technology, 37*(2), 22–25.

Herrington, J., & Oliver, R. (2000). An instructional design framework for authentic learning environments. *Educational Technology Research and Development, 48*(3), 23–48.

Hudson, R. F., Lane, H. B., & Pullen, P. C. (2011). Reading fluency assessment and instruction: What, Why, and How? *The Reading Teacher, 58*(8), 702–714.

Hutchison, A., & Woodward, L. (2014). A planning cycle for integrating digital technology into literacy instruction. *The Reading Teacher, 67*(6), 455–464.

International Literacy Association. (2018). *Standards for the preparation of literacy professionals 2017*. Newark, DE: Author.

International Society for Technology in Education. (2016). *ISTE standards for students*. Retrieved from https://www.iste.org/standards/for-students

Israel, S. E. (2017). *Handbook of research on reading comprehension* (2nd ed.). New York, NY: Guilford Press.

Jewitt, C. (2014). An introduction to multimodality. In C. Jewitt (Ed.), *The Routledge Handbook of Multimodal Analysis* (2nd ed.) (pp. 15–30). London, UK: Routledge.

Karchmer-Klein, R. (2007). Re-examining the practicum placement: How to leverage technology to prepare preservice teachers for the demands of the 21st century. *Journal of Computing in Teacher Education, 23*(4), 121–129.

Karchmer-Klein, R., Mouza, C., Shinas, V., & Park, S. (2017). Patterns in teachers' instructional design when integrating apps in middle school content area teaching. *Journal of Digital Learning in Teacher Education, 33*(3), 91–102.

Karchmer-Klein, R., & Pytash, K. E. (Eds.). (2020). *Effective practices in online teacher preparation for literacy educators*. Hershey, PA: IGI Global.

Karchmer-Klein, R., & Shinas, V. (2019). Adolescents' navigation of linguistic and non-linguistic modes in a digital narrative. *Journal of Research in Reading, 42*(3-4), 469–484. doi:10.1111/1467-9817.12278

Karpova, E., Correia, A, & Baran, E. (2009). Learn to use and use to learn: Technology in virtual collaboration experience. *Internet and Higher Education, 12*, 42–52.

Ko, S., & Rossen, S. (2017). *Teaching Online: A Practical Guide* (4th ed). New York, NY: Routledge.

Kulowiec, G. (2013). App Smashing Part I. [Blog post] Retrieved from kulowiectech .blogspot.com/2013/02/app-smashing-part-i.html

Lapp, D., Fisher, D., & Grant, G. (2008). "You can read this text—I'll show you how": Interactive comprehension instruction. *Journal of Adolescent & Adult Literacy, 51*(5), 372–383.

Liu, N. F., & Carless, D. (2006). Peer feedback: The learning element of peer assessment. *Teaching in Higher Education, 11*(3), 279–290.

Lu, H. (2010). Research on peer coaching in preservice teacher education—A review of literature. *Teaching and Teacher Education, 26*, 748–753.

Lundstrom, K., & Baker, W. (2009). To give is better than to receive: The benefits of peer review to the reviewer's own writing. *Journal of Second Language Writing, 18*, 30–43.

Luo, H., Koszalka, T. A., Arnone, M. P., & Choi, I. (2018). Applying case-based method in designing self-directed online instruction: A formative research study. *Education Technology Research Development, 66*(2), 515–544.

MacArthur, C. A. (2016). Instruction in evaluation and revision. In C. A. MacArthur, S. Graham, & J. Fitzgerald (Eds.), *Handbook of writing research* (2nd ed.) (pp. 272–287). New York, NY: Guilford.

Massumi, B. (2002). *Parables for the virtual: Movement, affect, sensation.* Durham, NC: Duke University Press.

McKeown, R. G., & Gentilucci, J. L. (2007). Think-aloud strategy: Metacognitive development and monitoring comprehension in the middle school second-language classroom. *Journal of Adolescent & Adult Literacy, 51*(2), 136–147.

Migyanka, J. M., Policastro, C., & Lui, G. (2005). Using a think-aloud with diverse students: Three primary grade students experience Chrysanthemum. *Early Childhood Education Journal, 33*(3), 171–177.

Mills, K. & Exley, B. (2014). Narrative and multimodality in English Language Arts curricula: A tale of two nations. *Language Arts, 92*(2), 136–143.

Mosley Wetzel, M., Maloch, B., Hoffman, J. V., Taylor, L. A., Vlach, S. K., & Greeter, E. (2015). Developing mentoring practices through video-focused responsive discourse analysis. *Literacy Research: Theory, Method, and Practice, 64*(1), 359–378. doi.org/10.1177/2381336915617611

National Council for the Social Studies. (2016). Media literacy. *Social Education 80*(3), 183–185.

National Council of Teachers of English. (2018). Beliefs for integrating technology into the English language arts classroom. Retrieved from www2.ncte.org/statement/beliefs-technology-preparation-english-teachers/

Neuman, S.B., & Dickinson, D.K. (2011). *Handbook of early literacy research* (Vol. 3). New York, NY: Guilford.

New London Group. (1996). A pedagogy of multiliteracies: Designing social futures. *Harvard Educational Review, 66*(1), 60–92.

Ogle, D. (1986). K-W-L: A teaching model that develops active reading of expository text. *The Reading Teacher, 39*, 564–570.

Oleson, A., & Hora, M. T. (2014). Teaching the way they were taught? Revisiting the sources of teaching knowledge and the role of prior experience in shaping faculty teaching practices. *Higher Education, 68*(1), 29–45.

Ortlieb, E., & Norris, M. R. (2012). Using the Think-Aloud strategy to bolster reading comprehension of science concepts. *Current Issues in Education, 15*(1), 1–8. Retrieved from cie.asu.edu/ojs/index.php/cieatasu/article/view/890/280

Philippakos, Z. A., & MacArthur, C. A. (2014, February). *The effects of giving feedback, using genre-specific evaluation criteria, on the quality of persuasive essays written by fourth and fifth-grade students.* Paper presented at the Writing Research Across Borders conference, Paris, France.

Pressley, M., & Afflerbach, P. (1995). *Verbal protocols of reading: The nature of constructively responsive reading.* Hillsdale, NJ: Lawrence Erlbaum.

Ronfeldt, M., Reininger, M., & Kwok, A. (2013). Recruitment or preparation? Investigating the effects of teacher characteristics and student teaching. *Journal of Teacher Education, 64*(4), 319–337.

Scheeler, M. C., Budin, S., & Markelz, A. (2016). The role of teacher preparation in promoting evidence-based practice in schools. *Learning Disabilities: A Contemporary Journal, 14*(2), 171–187.

Showers, B., & Joyce, B. (1996). The evolution of peer coaching. *Educational leadership, 53,* 12–16.

Shulman, L.S. (1986). Those who understand: Knowledge growth in teaching. *Educational Researcher, 15*(2), 4–14.

Smith, L. A. (2006). Think-aloud mysteries: Using structured, sentence-by-sentence text passages to teach comprehension strategies. *The Reading Teacher, 59*(8), 764–773.

Soisangwarn, A., & Wongwanich, S. (2014). Promoting the reflective teacher through peer coaching to improve teaching skills. *Procedia—Social and Behavioral Sciences, 116,* 2504–2511.

Soslau, E., Gallo-Fox, J., & Scantlebury, K. (2018). The promises and realities of implementing a coteaching model of student teaching. *Journal of Teacher Education.* Retrieved from journals.sagepub.com/doi/10.1177/0022487117750126

Straumsheim, C., Jaschik, S., & Lederman, D. (2015). *Faculty attitudes on technology.* Washington, DC: Inside Higher Ed and Gallup.

Tracey, D. H., & Morrow, L. M. (2017). *Lenses on reading: An introduction to theories and models.* New York, NY: Guilford Press.

U. S. Department of Education. (2010). Evaluation of evidence-based practices in online learning: A meta-analysis and review of online learning studies. Retrieved from www2.ed.gov/rschstat/eval/tech/evidence-based-practices/finalreport.pdf

U.S. Department of Education. (2016). *Future ready learning: Reimagining the role of technology in education.* Washington, DC: Office of Educational Technology.

Valencia, S. W., Martin, S. D., Place, N. A., & Grossman, P. (2009). Complex interactions in student teaching: Lost opportunities for learning. *Journal of Teacher Education, 60*(3), 304–322. doi:10.1177/0022487109336543

VanDerHeide, J., & Newell, G. E. (2013). Instructional chains as a method for examining the teaching and learning of argumentative writing in classrooms. *Written Communication, 30*(3), 300–329.

van Popta, E., Kral, M., Camp, G., Martens, R. L., & Simons, P. R.-J. (2017). Exploring the value of peer feedback in online learning for the provider. *Educational Research Review, 20,* 24–34.

Vygotsky, L. S. (1978). *Mind in Society: The development of higher psychological processes*. Cambridge, MA: MIT Press.

White, A. (2016). Using digital think alouds to build comprehension of online informational text. *The Reading Teacher, 69*(4), 421–425.

Zeichner, K. (2012). The turn once again toward practice-based teacher education. *Journal of Teacher Education, 63*(5), 376–382. doi:10.1177/0022487112445789

Index

About the Author

Rachel Karchmer-Klein, PhD, is an associate professor at the University of Delaware where she teaches undergraduate, graduate, and doctoral level courses in literacy and educational technology. She earned her doctorate in reading education at Syracuse University. Previously a classroom teacher and reading specialist, Dr. Karchmer-Klein began her university career at Virginia Commonwealth University. Her research investigates relationships among literacy skills, digital tools, and teacher preparation, with particular emphasis on technology-infused instructional design. Her overall goal is to improve preservice and practicing teachers' knowledge of how to leverage technological affordances to support students' literacy learning. Dr. Karchmer-Klein's work initially focused on K–12 instructional practices and has now expanded to include research on university faculty's use of technology in online course design. She taught her first fully online course in 2003 and now coordinates and teaches in two fully online graduate programs in education.